And The Band Plays On

The Life Story of
Larry Dodson of The Bar-Kays

And The Band Plays On

The Life Story of
Larry Dodson of The Bar-Kays

by

Larry Dodson

Edited by Shelia E. Bell

Congratulatory Remarks

"Forty-seven years and 29 albums later...Man!!!! We have had a hell of a ride and still going strong. Our relationship is golden. As you often say, "Every man's journey is different." Here's wishing you the very best on your new journey." *James Alexander, Founder and original leader of The Bar-Kays*

"From the first time that I interacted 'spiritually' with Larry Dodson I saw, heard, and felt him as the "beginning" of the transition of The Bar-Kays from being an instrumental group to having and creating a new innovative vocal identity with Larry as this authentic, one–of–a–kind unique vocalist and rare performing artist! As I would meet and communicate with Larry, I knew there was something profoundly special about him (Not another one like the other one!)! Even though over the years we never had a chance to spend a lot of "one-on-one" time together, the times we shared were always good times (pleasurable and honorable) filled with intelligence and understanding. Larry possessed integrity – the *inner source and being* of The Bar-Kays. I knew this about them from their beginning. But I will ALWAYS remember Larry Dodson as a profoundly creative artistic rarity that elevated The Bar-Kays into the class of Phenomenal Artistic Entertainment Performers!!! He is an eternally highlighted part of the existence of the Stax and Memphis Sound. I am proud, humbled, and thankful to call Larry Dodson My Dear, Precious Friend." *Very Respectfully, Al Bell, CEO Al Bell Presents and Former President of Stax Records*

"What many artists and fans today may not realize is that Larry Dodson influenced some of the most prominent artists of our time. Prince, Michael Jackson, Rick James were not the first to wear risqué attire and engage in suggestive dancing. It was Larry Dodson doing it before them. His preparation is his separation...a consummate pro." *Bobby Harris, Leader/Founder, The Dazz Band*

"Mr. Dodson, for the years that we have worked together, it has been truly wonderful and great to me. I consider you a great, great friend and truly a wonderful brother. Thank you! Many Blessings." *Mark Bynum, Keyboard Player, Background Vocalist & Longtime Member of The Bar-Kays*

"Larry Dodson is truly the Funk Master! If you want to be educated in Funk Music, open your music dictionary and you will see Larry Dodson's face. He is a pioneer in this industry and one of the most humble entertainers I have ever had the pleasure to meet. To grow up seeing and to actually meeting and working with this phenomenal artist has truly been a gratifying experience. The Tom Joyner Foundation has depended on Larry to bring the lineup of "The Masters of Funk" show on the Tom Joyner Fantastic Voyage Cruise yearly and out of the many plus entertainers that we have booked within the last 18 years, "The Masters of Funk" continues to be one of the best shows on the cruise year after year." *Lou Calhoun, Senior Entertainment Director, Tom Joyner Morning Show/Reach Media Inc.*

"Larry, thanks for bringing the hits year after year and Larry you can't retire!! Funk will never be the same without you." *Robert Day, Background Singer for The Bar-Kays*

"Yo, Popz AKA Larry Dodson, Sr. Thank you for being my leader and mentor. Thank you for allowing me to be a part of greatness. There are so many layers to the man who God has blessed me to have as my Dad. You have Brother Dodson, the God-fearing, humble church choir member; Larry, Sr., the boss of our company; Pop the go to for money and/or advice; Mr. Dodson, the tireless community leader and head of his house; Larry, the great husband to my amazing mom; Larry Dodson, the lead singer of the legendary Bar-Kays, and finally my dad, the man who I love dearly, who loves me, our family, and himself last."

Larry Dodson, Jr., Sr. Booking Agent for La'Marie's Entertainment and Marketing Manager for The Bar-Kays

"Forty-seven years is a long time to be married! The road was rocky at the start but with God's blessings and directions, we became soul mates. It gets better with time. I love you forever and always!" *Marie Dodson-Wife*

"I have known Larry Dodson for many years and had the pleasure of performing with the second generation of The Bar-Kays. It has been an honor to be a part of the brick layers of Funk!" *Angelo Earl- Guitarist for The Bar-Kays*

"Thank you for gracing my house. You're like fine wine now. Keep on keeping on. God bless y'all and I wish you 50 more years." *Louis Gossett, Jr- Academy Award Winning Actor*

"Dear Friend, you and I have shared a bond of friendship for more than 30 years. We started our friendship as casual acquaintances and the relationship developed into a stronger form of interpersonal bond than an association. I treasure those moments of having this opportunity to be friends as we are today. Later on in life, you took me under your leadership and guidance in the music industry and gave me an enormous boost with my career as Crew, Stage, Production, Road Manager as well as Tour Manager. Larry, you have been that person who paved the way for people in the music industry through performance, dedication, and commitment! "Reaching one's plateau in life simply defines your milestone." *Randy Hodges- Road Manager for The Bar-Kays*

"Larry and I go way back to when the snake was on tour with The Bar-Kays. Yep, Larry walked around with a huge snake. The Bar-Kays were performing on stage at a small club in Dallas and one night the snake got loose and crawled into a hole. Larry yelled out that his snake was missing and that was the end of the show...and the club. The group went in the club and never came back! The Bar-Kays are a classic funk band and Larry is a classic funk performer who never goes out of style." *Tom Joyner-Radio personality, Philanthropist, Activist*

"This is a band that has influenced many many bands of today and yesterday. God Bless you and your continued success." *Chaka Khan, ten time Grammy Award Winning Singer/Songwriter*

"What an honor it is to know Larry Dodson, a true music pioneer and legendary vocalist as the frontman for The Bar-Kays. I was so honored to meet you when I first got a chance to open up for various old school concerts. I never knew in a million years that I would be performing and sharing the stage with you. May God bless you, Larry. Love ya man!" *J. Lamont, Comedian*

"What started as an artist/business relationship evolved into a family relationship through the years as our mutual love for creating music connected us into a bond that could never be broken. That means a lot to both my wife Lillie and me. We both Love You!" *Archie and Lillie. Archie Love-Background Singer for The Bar-Kays and artist on the JEA/Rightnow Records label*

"There are but a few voices that one would consider to be signature only to them...Larry Dodson. There are no copies to the soulfulness, the sound, the power of this vocal superstar. True signature of Stax Records. The Memphis Sound!" *David Porter- Producer and Songwriter*

"I have been a fan of The Bar-Kays since their hit soundtrack theme "Shaft" which featured Isaac Hayes. When The Bar-Kays added lead singer Larry Dodson to their group, they became one of the most exciting groups that ever hit a live stage. Larry Dodson was a perfect match for The Bar-Kays. His entertaining energy and strong vocal ability would drive the band. I was blessed to develop a relationship with Larry. Everything about Larry says STAR, and he has STAR power. He is amazing, kind hearted, giving, and can really entertain!" *Abdul Ra'oof-Leader and Trumpet Player for The SOS Band*

"Larry, My hat goes off to you, my brother! I'm overseas now and I heard about your retirement party and I wish I could have been with you. I have so much respect for you and your work. Through the ups and downs, the under pay, you've been through it all like we all have. I just want you to know I love you man for you and your friendship to me and the things you have done with and without The Bar-Kays. May God continue to bless you and your family." *Bobby Rush, Grammy Award Winning Blues Artist*

"Mr. Dodson, or Popz, as most of us under his wings call him, has been so inspirational in my life as a musician and a person. He not only made me a better musician on stage, he taught me how to have class and professionalism offstage as well. I love this guy and I am forever indebted. Thank you for everything, Katt!" *Ezra "EZ Roc" Williams, Musical Director, Keyboard Player, Co-Producer for The Bar-Kays*

Dedication

First, I must give thanks to the Lord and Savior of my life, Jesus Christ, who has given me the strength and endurance to lead this incredible band, The Bar-Kays, for 47 years.

I dedicate this book to the three most important people in my life; my wonderful wife of 47 years, Marie; my daughter and my biggest fan, Precious; and the young man who pushes me every day and gets every ounce of energy that I have left to give to the music business, my incredible son, Larry, Jr.

It is because of these three people that I have gotten through the peaks and valleys of my long career. When I did everything wrong, they were patient with me. They have endured the bad times with me and helped me through it with unending patience and warm smiles when I needed them most. When I did everything right, they were the first to applaud me for all of the right reasons. They are now and have always been truthful with me, even when the truth may have cut like a knife.

Because of these three incredible human beings in my life, I am a much better man. I can truthfully say, without hesitation, they are the real reason why I now have a better relationship with God.

Finally, I know for sure that these three people know that my journey with The Bar-Kays has ended but "The Band Plays On".

Acknowledgements

I would be remiss and totally disrespectful if I did not begin at the beginning and acknowledge several very important people who are responsible for me being able to have been a part of this phenomenal musical journey.

The first person is Allen Jones who passed away a few years ago. It was Allen who saw the diamond in the rough in me, Larry Dodson. He gave me the opportunity to be the only lead singer The Bar-Kays would ever have. He believed in me when I often did not believe in myself. He made me study my craft, and taught me to love and respect this business we call 'show business.' Above all, he showed me the importance of remaining humble even though he knew that I would lead and others would follow.

The second person I would personally like to acknowledge is James Alexander, the only living original member of The Bar-Kays. James was man enough, wise enough, and had the perseverance to keep The Bar-Kays legacy alive after losing all of the members, but he and Ben Cauley in the unforeseen plane crash that took the life of Otis Redding. James allowed me to come into The Bar-Kays sacred space and give them a brand new beginning with my vocal ability. He stepped aside of the spotlight and allowed me to step into the spotlight where I remained for 47 years taking this band to new heights as he knew I would. His work ethics are unmatched by anyone that I know in this business, and I have learned a lot from him over the years. We have made a great team, James and I together as friends, business partners, and spiritual sounding boards for each other down through the years. Without these two incredible guys, there would not be a successful Larry Dodson, and that's pretty much for sure.

Lastly, to all of the members of The Bar-Kays band whom I consider some of the best guys, players, and people I've known in my life. Your loyalty to The Bar-Kays has been outstanding. I will never forget the many hours we've worked together and the many smiles we've left on the fans' faces after we've gone.

Yep, we rock!

I love you all and there's absolutely nothing you can ever do about it. Be well!

Popz

Why I Wrote "And the Band Plays On"

I must really be honest and admit that the real initial inspiration to write this book came from my son, Larry, Jr. who is probably the biggest Bar-Kays fan on planet earth. After hearing so many intriguing and personal Bar-Kays stories that I would often share with him, he would say to me, "Pops, you should write a book and let the world in on some of what you've shared with me. It would be amazing."

I began to think about what he said in the sense that what if people and the fans could get a chance to really know and understand what's it's really been like behind the scenes, to get the most personal backstage pass ever to see just what, how, and why things happened with Larry Dodson and The Bar-Kays. I think Larry, Jr. was right...it really could be amazing! So some 2 1/2 years ago I made the decision to write this book and tell this story as truthfully and as candidly as I could. I want all of the fans and readers to get to know me and what has made me tick all of these years. Also, I've always felt that there has been an unsung and somewhat brushed over attitude when it came to The Bar-Kays' career. So here again writing this book was a chance for me to get some things straight and make other things clearer about myself and the band.

"And the Band Plays On," would be a chance to show others what perseverance is really all about.

Lastly, in this book I have a chance to talk about the good, bad, and unfortunate things that have happened along the way in my life and in the long long life of the mighty Bar-Kays, (as Don Cornelius often call us on *Soul Train*.

After making the decision to retire (in 2017), I became even more driven to give the fans and readers more, as I knew my days were numbered and

2017 would be my last tour. I wanted them to share every moment as if they were there with me at every concert, as I said good-bye to one city at a time on tour, sharing every precious minute with me while *"the band plays on."*

And The Band Plays On

Larry Dodson

1

The Beginning of the Voice

I attribute my love of music to my father. He lived and breathed music, especially jazz. Listening to the music he played around the house, I began to identify the names of the artists and their various musical styles. I would go around the house singing, trying my best to imitate them.

Growing up, none of my three younger brothers (Jerry, Danny Ray, and my baby brother, Michael) were interested in music nor did they have a desire to sing like I did.

I guess I was around thirteen years old when I realized that I had a singing voice. Some evenings, after dinner, when it was my turn to clean up the kitchen, I would close the kitchen door and while I washed dishes I would sing some of my favorite songs by musical artists like Ray Charles, the Temptations, and Jerry Butler. It was fun, to say the least, imitating them and each of their unique styles.

I was more than intrigued by vocal groups. I was mesmerized by the way they performed, sounded, stepped, and dressed. Everything about them amazed me. During my teen years, my two favorite groups were The Temptations and Delfonics.

I loved to imitate singers and when I realized that I could use my voice for other enjoyable fun things like getting girls, it was on! Therefore, when I started having girlfriends, one of my favorite things to do was sing to them over the telephone. I would lay the telephone down on my bunk bed and sing sometimes for hours at a time or until my parents made me get off the phone. Yes, the girls loved it! I think that's when knew I was on to something and that I had talent.

By the time I started high school, the word had gotten around that I could sing. I started entering and singing at all of the school talent shows. I was always a big hit. I began thinking that maybe, just maybe, something good could happen if I used my voice to sing. At the time, I had no idea how right I was.

There were several singing groups around schools in the city that were known as doo-wop groups. Doo-wop was a type of music that was basically popular in African-American communities and consisted of an almost perfect vocal harmony with a mixture of Pop and R&B. The lyrics were on point and had a way of connecting with its listeners because of their simplicity and realness.

The more I became involved with music and singing, the more confidence I gained in myself and my talents so much so that I made a decision to start my own vocal doo-wop group.

I set out to find the perfect members for the group. I was fortunate to find two classmates who quickly shared in my dream—Deljuan Calvin had one of the sweetest, most unforgettable, falsetto voices I had ever heard, and Jasper "Jaboe" Phillips. The three of us became known as The Temprees. We came up with The Temprees from our absolutely crazy love of The Temptations. They were our idol group. Hell, we would have been The Temptations if that was possible. Since it wasn't, we made our group similar to The Temptations. I was a replica of David Ruffin and Paul Williams. Deljuan was Eddie Kendricks, and without a doubt Jaboe was a mixture of all of them.

Later, we added a fourth member and classmate to the group, Harold "Scotty" Scott. Scotty was an extremely popular guy around school, and the freshest dressing guy in the group. He made sure that we dressed to the max (as much as we could afford in those days), while I pushed for us to rehearse and sought gigs where we could perform.

Soon, The Temprees began to enter talent shows, sing at proms, and perform at other special events. We quickly became one of the favorite vocal groups around high schools in Memphis. The girls loved us and the other doo-wop groups respected us. Even the senior groups had to tip their hats to us. They couldn't deny the fact that there was something special about our voices.

Word got around the city that The Temprees were good and we developed a following. We were only teens but we began to receive offers to perform in nightclubs. Our parents believed in us so much that they signed documents that assured club owners that we would maintain good grades, stay away from liquor and drugs, and stay in our dressing rooms until it was time for us to perform. We adhered to these stipulations, for a while.

Wednesdays nights were the live nights in Memphis for the club scene. There was live music and performances in all of the clubs. We would divide the night up and do an early set at one club, leave that club, and then go to our regular gig.

We started out by performing at Club Showcase, and then we performed at Club Living Room and Club Down Under. Sometimes we would play a set at Club Down Under and at eleven o'clock we would be at Club Living Room, then leave there and play at another club, Club Rosewood. Occasionally, we would even do an after hour late late set at Club Down Under because it stayed open until five in the morning.

We made on average five dollars a man at each club, and that was only if we didn't eat or drink anything.

Soon we got a steady gig playing at Club Hippodrome. Club Hippodrome was where all of the big time entertainers played. The Temprees performed every Monday, Wednesday, and Friday nights from ten until two in the morning, and sometimes later on the weekends. Mind you, we were still in high school when all of this was going on!

While playing at the clubs, older women started coming on to us. They offered us money and as long as we hung out with them we hardly ever had to pay for anything. The only thing about them was that they were quite possessive and 'branded' us like we were cattle.

Some of the women wanted us to spend the night with them. It was hard to turn them down so most of the time we took them up on their offers. They definitely 'broke us in'.

As for my parents, they trusted me and so did the parents of the other guys in the group. My parents gave me more latitude than I probably should have had at my age, but they liked the idea of me being popular.

When I stayed out all night, I would tell my parents that I stayed over Jaboe's house or Scotty's house or Deljuan's house. The same thing went for Jaboe, Scotty, and Deljuan. We covered each other and kept our scripts together. Plus, there were times when we didn't leave the club until four or five o'clock in the morning so it was easy to lie and say that we had to perform all night.

We became quite promiscuous. There were nights at the clubs when there were so many tables of different women that we were fooling around with that we had to sneak out after we finished our set in order to avoid problems.

Living the type of lifestyle that we were living at such an early age was wild and crazy but we loved every minute of it. The girls at school loved us, the older women loved us, and other groups totally respected us for our drive and success.

It felt good to know that I had created The Temprees, so all of the notoriety and love we received throughout Memphis and the mid-south was like icing on a cake.

It wasn't long before The Temprees started getting noticed by local record labels that wanted to record us. Two of our managers were Deanne Parker and her boyfriend, Randle Catron. Deanne wrote a song for The Temprees called "I Wanna Load You Up" and we were going to audition for Stax. If we had gotten accepted at Stax this would be the song we planned to record. Unfortunately, it never came into fruition.

Deanne Parker, however, went on to become the first female to be recorded at Stax Records and eventually the well-known publicist for Stax.

5

There was another local label owned by a guy who worked across the street from Stax at a record shop. We tried to get on his label, too but again The Temprees were unsuccessful. It just wasn't our time and who knows what would have happened if we had been signed. Maybe I wouldn't have had the opportunity with The Bar-Kays that unknowingly was forthcoming. Yep, it's true—God definitely does work in mysterious ways.

2

When Tragedy Strikes

I idolized The Bar-Kays as a group. Don't get me wrong, I was obsessed with The Temptations, but from a local standpoint The Bar-Kays were at the top of the chain even though I didn't know them well. They had the number one record in the country, "Soulfinger" and they were still in high school just like The Temprees! In our eyesight they had made it. They were hot and they were sharp. And no way would they play behind The Temprees; they were too big for that.

The Bar-Kays were backing Otis Redding, one of the greatest singers to ever grace the stage. I remember where I was the day I heard the tragic news about them and Otis Redding.

As I said earlier, me and the guys in The Temprees messed around with older women. There were these two chicks who we hung out with—Evelyn and Mary were their names.

I will never forget that day. It was December 10, 1967. It was memorable, not because we were hanging out, kicking it and having a good time with Evelyn and Mary, but because of the horrible tragedy that shook the city of Memphis that day.

Me and the rest of the guys were chilling at Evelyn and Mary's apartment when a news flash came on the television saying that the plane Otis Redding and The Bar-Kays were on had gone down. They suspected all aboard the plane were killed.

I got on the telephone immediately and started to call around to see if it was really true and to get some more information, but nobody knew much more than what the news stated. It all came out later, bit by bit, and it was the most tragic news Memphis had ever experienced.

Redding, along with The Bar-Kays, had left what would be his final recording session in Memphis to go make a television appearance in Cleveland, Ohio and then he had to perform in Madison, Wisconsin. On his way to Madison the private plane he and The Bar-Kays were on crashed into the frigid waters of Lake Monona, just three miles from the Madison airport. It was one of the saddest days of my life.

The Bar-Kays were my idols and Memphis' pride and joy, not just because of their musical contributions but because they symbolized a certain kind of spiritual connection for Memphis, which is hard to put into words. They carried the torch for Memphis wherever they went, and were the epitome of the Memphis sound. They conquered the racial divide without even giving it a second thought by having Ronnie Caldwell, a white kid in the band, who left his all-white school to transfer to Booker T. Washington High School just to be closer to them. Ronnie loved them just that much.

James often said that Ronnie Caldwell was the only white kid he knew who could walk through Foote Homes Projects, which during that time was the heart of the black ghetto, holding hands with his black girlfriend. Mind you, no one would say a word to him about it. Truly amazing!

The Bar-Kays trumpet player, Ben Cauley, went down with the plane but thank God he survived. Carl Sims, another guy who was the singer they sometimes used on gigs, and James Alexander also dodged the bullet, so to speak, because they had stayed behind and were going to take a commercial flight. It just wasn't their time.

We cried almost an hour after learning of their deaths. I thought that Memphis and the entire music community would never get over this tragic loss.

3

In the Beginning

No matter where I was going or coming from, whether it was from a girlfriend's house, a friend's house, or wherever, if I rode the bus I would have to ride downtown and then transfer to a 31 Crosstown Kansas bus in order to get back home.

Several times, there was this rather short, thin, dark-skinned guy at the bus stop, too. I caught him staring at me a time or two like he was trying to figure out whether he knew me or not. I noticed that he transferred to the 8 Chelsea bus, which meant he probably lived in, or was going to, North Memphis for whatever reason.

After seeing him at the bus stop a few times, he struck up a conversation with me. He told me he had heard of my group, The Temprees. That wasn't much of a surprise because The Temprees were quite well known throughout the city. Whether we were together as a group or alone, there was usually someone somewhere that recognized us.

I wasn't too bothered by him because he seemed harmless so I conducted a normal conversation with him. He would ask me how I was doing and how The Temprees were doing, which was cool. On one occasion, while I waited to transfer, we talked and he asked me a few questions including a question about The Bar-Kays. He wanted to know if I liked their music, and of course I told him that I did. Keep in mind, this was after the tragedy that killed the original Bar-Kays. The group had rebirthed and had members who took the place of those that died that tragic day. Anyway, we talked and I answered most of his questions and then went about my way; he did the same.

On another occasion when I saw him, out of the blue he said to me, "One day I'm gonna get you". I thought that was the weirdest thing in the world for some strange dude to say but I shrugged it off and again transferred to my bus and went about my business.

It wasn't until much later that I found out that I had been talking to Allen Jones, songwriter and producer for Stax Records! Most of all, Allen was the closest thing to being the manager of The Bar-Kays as anyone could be at that time. Little did I know, but he had been watching my performances with The Temprees for quite some time and sizing me up for a frontman for The Bar-Kays.

I discovered who he was when The Temprees went to audition at Stax. When I walked into the studio, I saw him and that's when I learned who he was. Talking about being surprised, I was.

One Sunday night, a few months after our unsuccessful audition at Stax, The Temprees were performing at Club Showcase when James Alexander of The Bar-Kays came to the show. Between sets, he walked up, pulled me to the side, and asked if he could talk to me for a minute. James didn't beat around the bush. He asked me if I would be interested in leaving The Temprees and joining The Bar-Kays as their lead singer. He told me that The Bar-Kays were changing their style and were going from being an instrumental band to a vocal group. My heart not only skipped a beat, but it almost popped out of my chest!

I was overwhelmed at the thought of being the frontman and lead singer for the band that I, along with millions of people all over the world, loved. Not that I didn't feel something for The Temprees, the group I started and also loved, but joining The Bar-Kays was a chance for me to get into the big time.

I admit, I was afraid because I didn't know if I would be able to handle being their lead singer, so immediately I started to second guess myself. Nevertheless, I told James that I was interested but I needed some time to think it over.

After a few days of going without sleep, wondering how I was going to deal with the whole situation and what I would say to my group if I chose to leave, I called James and accepted the offer. After that, I told the guys in my group about my decision.

One night, during one of The Temprees' final performances, we were in the wings waiting to go on when Deljuan snapped and started pounding me in the back of my head like he was crazy. I guess he was angry because I decided to leave the group, so he let it out on me right then and there. We fought until Scotty and Jaboe pulled us apart, and then we went on stage. Believe it or not, we had a great show that night. It was one of the last times we performed together as The Temprees.

About two or three years after I had been in The Bar-Kays, The Temprees returned to Stax Records and recorded through one of its affiliated labels called We Produce. That began a long and fruitful recording career for them with a string of hits that included "Love Maze", "If I Could Say What's On My Mind", "I'm For You, You For Me", "Dedicated To the One I Love", and many more. They became labeled as the love men because of their slow jam releases.

I remain grateful for the vision I had to start The Temprees and for their fortitude to keep the group going after I moved on to my new role with The Bar-Kays.

4

The Idol Maker

After accepting the offer to be the lead singer for The Bar-Kays, I was totally taken off guard when I realized that I was not exactly one of the favorite persons in the band. I found out later that there were other choices that some of the guys had for the lead singer who they believed were actually better and more experienced than me, but Allen Jones had obviously pushed the band to bring me on.

Allen had a vision for the group that they didn't see or understand. I would later come to realize that Allen was not just a manager, but a manager, visionary and idol maker, all rolled into one. He recognized that the other guys would not listen to him, respect him or his vision, and certainly would not be candidates to follow the directions that he had planned for the band to carry out.

When Allen started to talk to us about the new image he wanted for the group, we all looked at each other with our mouths wide open because some of the things he wanted us to do, some of the outfits he wanted us to wear, some of the songs he wanted us to sing and play were the total opposite of our characters. In some cases it appeared feminine, especially for me as the lead singer.

Nevertheless, the new Bar-Kays emerged with a band made up of a spaced out looking bunch of black kids with me in front as this wildly dressed, Sly Stone influenced, black rock, over the top, lead singer.

The record label thought we had lost our freaking minds, that we must have been getting high and couldn't make good decisions about our music and style of dress. Our image was everything but somehow the people began to find us mysterious, innovative, wild, and intriguing. Although we didn't have hit records, we put on a hell of a show!

Allen made us rehearse ten to twelve hours almost every day. We were deadly tight with incredible arrangements to popular Rock and R&B songs that we uniquely blended Rock, Funk, and R&B overtones into.

My first few months in The Bar-Kays was all about finding my way into this brand new life Allen Jones was creating for me. There were times I felt like the guys really wished that I would just pack my shit up and leave.

There was James Alexander, the leader of the band, who was like a captain respectfully carrying out the orders of the general, Allen. James, on Allen's orders, may have invited me to join The Bar-Kays but he never thought I was much of a singer and never saw what Allen saw in me. It did hurt my feelings that he didn't think I was good enough for the job. The good thing is we both got over it after I started recording and doing shows. It didn't hurt that the girls and guys really started to dig me as the new lead singer for The Bar-Kays.

Ben Cauley, an incredible trumpet player and the only member to survive the plane crash, was known for two things by the group—he was always going to be well-dressed and he was always late for everything. He would make a dramatic appearance into the club after the band had already started playing without him. He would come in, march down the middle of the club, fully dressed in his uniform, twirling his trumpet around and around (something he became known for), and the crowd would go crazy, but the band would be furious.

Then there was Harvey, the saxophone player, one of the older, more arrogant but wise members in the band. Harvey came from a clone band of The Bar-Kays called The Wildcats.

The Wildcats played and knew every song in The Bar-Kays' show. They often took the gigs The Bar-Kays could not play. Harvey had little to say to me or anyone. He wasn't a very good sax player but he was an intelligent guy and adding to that a very good songwriter.

The same as he felt about me, James didn't agree with Allen's reason for picking Harvey to play in The Bar-Kays when he already had such a good trumpet player in Ben. But Allen saw something else in Harvey—his size. You see, Harvey weighed about 100 pounds and looked great in everything he wore. He could make a simple pair of jeans look like they came from Italy when he put them on with just a simple shirt because of his size and build. I was slim and lean, too and a nice looking guy as well. Allen's visual dream slowly began to make sense.

Winston Stewart, the keyboard player, was hired one month before me. This really blew James' mind because Winston wasn't a seasoned keyboard player at all. He was quiet, and much like me, he tried to get along with everyone. Certainly, in James' mind, he was not Bar-Kays material.

Michael Toler was a fifteen-year old kid and the guitar player. He was the closest thing to a musical genius that I had ever seen as a guitar player. He lived and breathed to play the guitar and was a great choice for The Bar-Kays. His mother was a soothsayer or palm reader and just an overall strange lady; so was Mike in many ways. He would lock himself in a room or on the tour bus bathroom for hours at a time and practice his guitar. No girls. No drugs. No drinking. Nothing but his guitar in his life. On stage, and in the studio, he was the shit!

Willie Hall was the drummer and another very strange bird. He smoked a lot of weed, was very opinionated, always disagreed with Allen, and like Ben he was always late. Overall, Willie was just the guy in the band. He was funny, too and kept us laughing, especially when he was high, which was all the time. He was the one guy Allen could not control.

My first gig with the band was at the Holiday Inn Ballroom. I didn't have a uniform so Allen put me one together, which later came to be one of my signature stage ensembles. It consisted of painted leotards, tall white marching band boots, a chain vest, and a headband. I sang three or four songs that night. "Knock on Wood" was one of them. That was in the fall of 1970, some 47 years ago. Wow...*and the band plays on.*

5

On The Road

Being on the road with The Bar-Kays felt a little weird at first, because as I said, none of the guys really liked me, especially after I started to get a little attention, which they had not been used to sharing.

Allen worked hard to create a style for me not just visually, but vocally. It all started to come together on tape and on stage. On stage I was somewhere between Mick Jagger, Tina Turner, Sly Stone, and David Bowie. On tape I was still searching for my own identity, but I guess you could say I was a mixture of Joe Cocker, Ray Charles, Sly Stone, and two or three other screaming white boys who were popular at the time.

We were recording a really cool cut but often confusing mixtures of soul, funk, and rock with long arrangements similar to Blood, Sweat, and Tears and other white groups. We were totally influenced by Sly

18

and The Family Stone, really over influenced to be honest, but hey, *the band plays on.*

My first single recording with the band actually didn't feature me as lead. It was called "Sang and Dance". We all had singing lines in the song like Sly and The Family Stone, but the song didn't fare well. It later became sampled by Will Smith for his huge smash "Get Jiggy Wit It". To this day it has paid us the most royalties we've earned from a single. The "Black Rock" album was my first full-length album recording with the band. To this day, it remains one of my favorite albums we ever recorded. It was an incredible fusion of soul, R&B, rock, and jazz combined with heavy arrangements that no other black group was doing.

I spent many nights at home pondering how I would ever get through such an incredible undertaking. Thanks to our incredible producer, Allen, I made it and we made it! That album challenged every fiber of my being to reach the bar Allen set for me as the new, never before heard voice of The Bar-Kays. Not only did I get through it, but I discovered a new Larry Dodson, vocally.

I may not have been much of a singer but there was something about the raspy, honest, churchy, soulful vocal I possessed that was interesting, unique, and often moving to listen to. We recorded cover songs like "You Don't Know Like I Know" by Sam and Dave, "Baby I Love You" by Aretha Franklin, "I've Been Trying" by The Impressions and Curtis Mayfield. We were able to breathe new life into their already iconic songs by rocking them up.

As much as I liked the "Black Rock" album, and as proud as we were when we finally finished it, the record label didn't think much of it. To create an album so far from our soulful R&B roots, they thought we were too far out in left field and that we had lost our minds. However, inside the company, our fellow label mates applauded us. They admired our guts. They kind of labeled us "The Bad Boys of Stax Records" and we totally lived up to that nickname in every sense of the word. Our music, our dress, and our attitude said we were the next best thing—catch up world!

We worked the clubs around town and always had large crowds when we performed. We took some overseas gigs in Japan, too.

In between gigs, James, Ben, Willie, and Michael did a lot of session work around Stax for Rufus and Carla Thomas, Albert King, Johnny Taylor, Staple Singers, The Emotions, and William Bell. They made R&B history by playing on songs like "Cheaper to Keep Her" by Johnny Taylor, "I'll Play The Blues For You" by Albert King, "Pork Salad Annie" by Tony Joe White, The Emotions first single "So I Can Love You", and hundreds of other incredible and iconic R&B hits.

Booker T and the MG's had gotten rich and were leaving a lot of room for The Bar-Kays to come in and catch sessions that they would normally play on. The most popular being Isaac Hayes. James and the rhythm section worked on his first album, "Hot Buttered Soul", and it took up a lot of their time.

Meanwhile, we toured as much as we could. I was quickly becoming the well-known new lead singer who always wore red, white, and blue leotards, a Captain America long-fringed vest, which draped to the floor, and a red, white, and blue headband around my straight permed hair. My straight hair became my trademark all over the trade magazines. I was controversial. I was fresh. I was different. I was a unique voice for the band. Along with that, we began dressing stranger and stranger by the day. People were beginning to talk and wonder if we were gay because of our flamboyant style of dress. We were far from that, but Allen loved us involved in controversy.

Most of the guys in the band were somewhat uncomfortable with the feminine style of dress and outfits that Allen wanted us to wear but because of his unusual way of getting what he wanted out of us, convincing us to follow his lead in every inch of our career, we did just about everything that he asked.

Probably one of the biggest arguments Allen ever had was with Harvey over Harvey wearing a white wig that later became one of the band's stage ID's and visual trademarks.

Allen was an idol maker but we couldn't see it or believe it then. After all, we were all just a bunch of kids from the ghetto nervous about the idea of success and even more concerned or uncomfortable with putting our lives in the hands of another guy not much older than we were.

Allen was possessive, overprotective, and an overall controlling person who was slowly making us his life. He controlled all aspects of our music, money, stage dress, stage dialogue; he even controlled our weight!

Eventually, his control of us spilled over into our personal lives. He wanted to know everything about us and about anything in our personal lives that took time away from The Bar-Kays. He would give us such a guilt trip about not being dedicated enough to the band. This was good for us, in a sense, because Allen saw greatness and something special about The Bar-Kays, especially since the band had a singer to help breathe more life into the performances. Looking back, in retrospect, he had to have complete control over us until we could see the visions and dreams more clearly for ourselves.

6

Life Changes

In 1970, four months after I became part of The Bar-Kays, I married my beautiful high school sweetheart, Marie. Initially, we had no place of our own so we stayed with her parents, which was bad because there were five other girls living there, plus her brother, all in a five-room house.

Marie was a year older than me, much more mature and settled in her mind about things in life. I, on the other hand, was a young musician waiting for my big break. Mainly, at that time, I just wanted to earn enough money to support Marie and pay the few bills we had. I was making $75 a week with the band and Marie was working job-to-job to help make ends meet.

Less than a year later, we moved out of her parents' house and in with one of Marie's friends. We stayed there until we were able to get our own apartment.

Marie and I had a wonderful first year of marriage, but we got a terrible scare when I received a notice in the mail that I was classified high in eligibility to be drafted into the Army. In fact, several of the guys in the band got high classifications. The threat of being drafted became an elephant in the room and quite a scary thought because the Vietnam War was looming in the midst during that time.

Finally, it happened. James received a notice to report to the draft board for an examination, the first step into being drafted. Prior to any of us going down to the draft board, we made a vow that we would do whatever it took to get reclassified to get out of going to the service.

The day James went to the draft board he dressed in full band uniform, which consisted of black leotards, fur boots, a long-fringed vest, a Spanish Zorro type hat, dark sunglasses, and his bass guitar. We were at rehearsal when a call came from James. He said officials at the draft board were going to arrest him but he ran out of the building. He was calling from a phone booth and begging for someone to come and get him before they found him and caught him. He was high off angel dust and was completely out of his mind.

Allen went and picked him up and brought him to safety. After that, James was reclassified as 4F, the lowest classification you can get.

Next to receive a notice was me. I decided to take a similar plan as James—I dropped a couple of tokes of acid and smoked some angel dust. I was so high I thought it was the end of the line for me.

Marie promised she would take care of me during my acid trip, which I called myself timing to make sure I would be out of my mind by the time I was to report to the draft board.

I made it to the draft board the following day after having incredible hallucinations the night before that Marie was the devil in bed with me and that I had to get rid of her. Afraid that I was going to harm her for real, I jumped up, got out of the bed, and went to another room to make sure I wouldn't hurt her. I was scared to death. I had never been that high and out of my mind like that.

Marie took me to the draft board and like James, I wore my band outfit with a long bag hanging off my shoulder, a tam on my head, (a very feminine tam at that). I was going to pretend I was gay. Back then being gay would surely get me a 4F classification. They would get a woman before drafting a 4F classification. So, there I was sitting in the waiting room at the draft board high as a kite, nervous, paranoid, and quite scared of what the outcome of all of this would be.

While I was waiting, I began to notice everyone was being called except me. Finally, everyone had been seen and waited on and I was still left just sitting there. One of the sergeants came over and asked me my name and for my paperwork. When I gave it to him, he looked at me with a stern look and told me that I had reported on the wrong day. My appointment was not until the following day. Hearing this, I could have dropped dead right then and there!

I left the draft board and rushed to the phone to call Marie to come pick me up, hoping that no one would see me. Remember, I looked like a gay blonde and that could never get out to the public, even though it wasn't true at all. Now I needed to go home, get out of my get up, come down off of all the drugs, and do it all over again for the next day.

The next day, at the draft board, I answered what seemed like a million questions on the paperwork they gave me to complete. When it came to the question about my sexual preference I marked 'homosexual'. Of course that raised a red flag when the sergeant began to read my chart, but it didn't stop them from making me go through with all of the tests.

I pulled every stunt I could trying to fail, especially the hearing test, but the officer was on to me and made me take it all over again. Long story short—I finished the tests, ran out of the office like I was crazy, and later got a 4F classification which kept me out of the Armed Forces forever. I beat the draft!

7

The Mothership Connection

Marie and I remained happily married and very much in love. Life in The Bar-Kays continued to be a challenge because it was becoming ever more obvious that I was a big part of the future of The Bar-Kays from both the recording side and the live performance side.

Allen continued to be over possessive with the group. It was not healthy for the married guys or for the stronger willed like Ben. Willie, James, Harvey, Winston, and I were more easygoing and easier to deal with. We liked the controversy and perhaps trusted Allen more in general.

Our touring extended to traveling around Los Angeles, performing at clubs like the world famous Troubadour, Whisky A Go Go, PJ's, and other LA hot spots. We were rocking the house every night.

When we were approached by Al Bell, the Vice President of Stax Records, to perform at the Wattstax

Concert, our lives began to change both individually and as a band. This was just after the Watts Riots in Los Angeles. The concert was the brainchild of Al. It was his way of helping to calm things down.

Allen came up with this wild idea about how we could steal the show at Wattstax. We were to come out on stage on white horses with a white horse-driven gladiator chariot. Somehow, Isaac Hayes, who wasn't the headliner of the concert, got wind of our little scheme and sent word to the band that if we did that he would have us put off the show. He had just recorded the soundtrack for "Shaft" with The Bar-Kays, for which he received an Oscar. It was the first time in music history that a song from a movie had won an Oscar.

Not only did The Bar-Kays' stock go up by 200% after recording "Shaft" with Isaac, our popularity and respect was on the rise. As for me, my stock went up as well, being the crazy, skinny-legged, wild child with the straight hair, and raspy, raunchy voice.

Little did we know that our performance at Wattstax would turn out to be the largest audience we would ever perform in front of—100,000! The Bar-Kays stole the show with an electric 14-minute performance which included our own hit, "Son of Shaft".

When the movie *Wattstax* premiered, we attended the first screenings and premieres. We made such an impression in the movie until our performance was on the promo poster and in the track for the movie.

It was at the LA movie premiere of *Wattstax* where I was fortunate enough to take a picture with the actress Zsa Zsa Gabor. The picture began to circulate through the trade magazines, both black and white. Soon after, rumors started circulating that Zsa Zsa and I were dating. Good for publicity, but not as good

28

for my new wife, Marie. Although Marie trusted me, the rumor did make her raise an eyebrow or two. Of course, the rumors weren't true, but again, Allen loved the idea of such huge publicity.

The band started to do more recording with Isaac Hayes. We recorded his first five albums, which included "Hot Buttered Soul", "Shaft", "Moses", and "To Be Continued". We were on a roll, but our albums were not being received like we wanted them to. On top of that, Stax Records was in huge financial trouble, mostly due to the fact of slow record sales from the artists. In addition, Al Bell had taken over as president of the label. He made a very bad deal with Columbia Records involving millions of dollars, which later was discovered as part of a deceitful trap to take control of Stax Records.

The Bar-Kays were hurting for money. We were turned down on all of the efforts we made to borrow money or get advances from the label.

Later, however, in 1976, came the huge success of "Shake Your Rump to The Funk". The Bar-Kays were on fire again. We began appearing on TV shows and our songs were constantly being played on the radio. All we needed now was a spot on a major tour.

George Clinton, leader of the highly successful group, Parliament-Funkadelic, was a good friend of James Alexander. We heard that they were going out on a major national tour so we sent James to Detroit to ask George, personally, for an opening spot.

James went to Detroit and found George in the studio recording and finally (he was nervous) got around to asking him for a spot on the tour. Without missing a beat, or thinking about it, George said, "Sure." James was so taken with the quick answer until he said, "George, quit playing. This is serious." George repeated it a little louder than the first time.

"I told you yes. It's cool." James couldn't believe what he was hearing so he asked him a third time and George shouted, "Man, look you're on the tour. Now get out of here!"

James brought the good news back to Memphis. When I tell you everything changed, I mean everything changed. The Bar-Kays not only got a spot on the tour, but George gave us a co-star spot and we came on just before he did.

We played about 85 dates. All of them sold out with the exception of about seven or eight. It was an incredible tour to watch Parliament-Funkadelic do their thing every night, land the Mothership live on stage, and to see George come out of the Mothership to make the crowd go absolutely bananas.

Not only did the tour put us in good financial shape, our fan base increased by one hundred percent. In addition to that, we made a deal with a concession guy who traveled with the tour and sold concessions for us. We made a killing, and so did George. Even today, when we see George, we always talk about the tour, which highly influenced the career of The Bar-Kays and the group, Cameo, who opened the show.

As years went by, George Clinton and I became close friends. He understood exactly what James and I were trying to do with The Bar-Kays and he respected how funky the band was and me as a stylist singer, the same as he was. George, Sly Stone, Rick James, and I all came from the same school.

Parliament-Funkadelic (P-Funk) was a heavy influence on the music and sound of The Bar-Kays. The band was now a ten-piece band. We added two more guys, Sherman Guy, a background singer and percussionist, and Mark Bynum, a keyboard player who helped to bring a new keyboard bass sound to the band on record and live performances.

Mark was a great background singer with a voice very close to mine. He really helped vocally on the live performances.

Both Mark and Sherman were instrumental in making the live versions of our records sound like the recorded version, something that was important to us. We believed in giving the fans one hundred percent in our live concerts. We were always thinking of new ways to spark the show up and keep it unpredictable.

8

Precious Precious

One of the most devastating and life-changing events in my life was the birth of our daughter. I was twenty-years old and Marie was twenty-one when our firstborn child and daughter came into the world. We named her "Precious".

Marie and I tried having a kid for a year with no success when, finally, she got pregnant. She began staying with her mom as she got closer to her delivery time. The Bar-Kays were still doing gigs, and toward the end of the pregnancy The Bar-Kays went to Japan on a two-month gig.

The band loved Tokyo, but it was the longest period we had been away from home so me and the rest of the guys in the band got pretty homesick. We played six days a week, four shows a night at Club Mugen, a highly popular club in Tokyo. We started at six that evening and would play until midnight. Afterwards, we would go to a private club, drink all night, and sleep all day the next day at the band house, which was a super nice four-bedroom apartment.

The Japanese were incredible people. The girls were very friendly and always buying us things. The yen was at an all-time high of 360, which equaled to about three dollars and a half to every one of our American dollars. We spent a lot while over there buying tailored leather suits, coats, you name it. I sent money home since I had a baby on the way.

We arrived back to the states after a successful tour, but something was brewing with Ben Cauley and Michael Toler. They were planning to leave the band and I could feel it. They both obviously had made their minds up while in Japan because they both quit after we got back to the United States. That hurt the band in many ways.

Ben and Mike were by far the most talented guys in the band so replacing them was a real task. As for the reason they left, I believe Ben left because we weren't making enough money to support his large family, and he and Allen never really saw eye to eye on a number of things. Ben never wanted Allen to have the kind of control over him like Allen had over the rest of us.

Mike, on the other hand, was just strange, a loner, an introvert, and a geek. It was never really clear at that time why he left, or should I say it was never clear to me.

After being home for a few weeks, my daughter was born after Marie went through eighteen hours labor. I can't explain it, but I had the strangest feeling about the pregnancy, especially during the last few months of Marie's pregnancy. Call it intuition or whatever, I just suspected something was wrong. Sure enough, the doctors came out to the

Father's Waiting Room the day Precious was born and told me that Marie had given birth to a baby girl. He assured me that Marie was fine but our little girl would have to remain in the hospital a few days for observation and tests.

In my mind, keeping our child for observation meant something was definitely wrong. I was right. Precious was born with a number of medical issues. The doctor later informed me and Marie that Precious had Down syndrome. He told us that children born with Down syndrome rarely lived past their teens. Of course, that was devastating for us.

We had no idea what to do, and we didn't tell our parents for a long time. Mostly, because we were ashamed, afraid of what people would say and do. Yet, one thing prevailed and that was the fact that she was our daughter whom we both loved dearly. We knew we would do whatever it took to get the most out of her life. The fact that the doctor said not to get too attached to our child was just garbage to me and Marie.

Through the years Precious had a number of challenges, like most Down syndrome kids, but by the grace of God she came through every one. As God would have the last word, as of the writing of this book, Precious has survived every ordeal that has come before her, including open-heart surgery to repair a hole in her heart the size of a silver dollar and a rare dislocated vertebra.

A vertebra in her neck was dislodging slowly toward her spine and could not be detected by regular X-rays. A German doctor by the name of Van Buren came to us and told us that he knew exactly what the problem was. He later operated on Precious and fused the vertebrae in her neck with a bone from another part of her body. For one week, she was in traction with a halo drilled in her skull, unable to move her head and upper body, but she never shed a tear. Doctors were so amazed that they would come into her room every morning to look at her because they couldn't understand how she withstood such tremendous pain at her age.

Marie couldn't stand to go into the room and see Precious in traction. She would burst into tears every time. Precious had to wear a half body cast. She did lose some movement in her neck and her body was a bit one-sided after wearing a heavy body cast for so long, but other than that, she fully recovered. The hospital staff said it was truly amazing; they said they had never seen anything like it before.

We were fortunate to be able, in later years, to afford to get her the best care, the best school tutors, and Precious progressed much better than the average Down syndrome kid. She has worked all of her adult life and at the time of this book, Precious is now 46 years old. She is truly a success story!

It would be eight years after Precious was born before Marie and I got up enough courage to have another kid. Larry Jr. was born July 12, 1979 with blue eyes. Can you believe that? Marie's side of the family had all nice looking girls and all of them were light-skinned and tall. My side of the family (or should I say my dad's side) was biracial. My father's mother, Grandmother Cole, was part American Indian; her sister was white. My dad had green eyes and Larry Jr. certainly had eyes like him.

Larry's eyes eventually changed from blue to green and finally to a light hazel blend. He was a gorgeous kid. We had to fight with our family members (in a good way) just to keep our own baby at home. They all loved to keep Larry, Jr., and of course Precious also stole every heart that she came in contact with.

Marie and I began to understand God's infinite wisdom and the fact that he never ever makes a mistake. Having Precious in our lives has been a wonderful blessing in so many ways. I know that may seem strange to say, but there have been so many life lessons that we have learned having a mentally challenged kid.

9

The Big Tour

One of the biggest tours we did was with Isaac Hayes during his hottest and most popular period after recording "Shaft". It lasted about 30 days and most of the concerts were sold out. Personally, I didn't enjoy it that much because we had to ride the tour bus with most of Isaac's band and they were a rough and rowdy bunch. A lot of them were on heavy drugs and for the most part were not our kind of people. We had no choice but to travel with them at the time because we couldn't afford to travel by ourselves on the money we were making.

Luther Ingram was the co-star on the tour, riding on his hit single, "If Loving You Is Wrong", (which ironically, we recorded years later as a duet with me and Evelyn "Champagne" King.) He smoked constantly and it really got in the way of his performance and his business time. I recall one night, after a concert, Luther was so stoned that he left $5,000 on the counter of a hotel we were staying at on the tour!

There was always a big crap game on the bus going on after the concerts, which Isaac Hayes' road manager and staff usually ended up getting the best of every night. If you were a real gambler, you could get in on the big games with the high stakes in the hotel room of Isaac's manager. I got in on it a couple of times only to quickly find out I was in the wrong place and in over my head.

When I was winning, they would not let me leave the room until I let them win back some of their money. That was the only way to get out of the room alive. Winning and then leaving was not allowed by rookies like me. These could be very dangerous, thuggish guys. I stopped gambling with them altogether to avoid trouble and to keep the peace.

Between the fall of 1968 and late 1970, we released a total of five singles. None of the 45's managed to dent the Pop or R&B charts.

In 1971, we were still struggling to come up with a decent single, and we did. We recorded "The Son of Shaft", a spinoff of "Shaft". It was a clever idea that Allen came up with, a similar arrangement spotlighting the wah wah guitar. Our horn section and I put a killer lead vocal on the track. The guitar was played by Vernon Burch, a fifteen-year old kid we picked up in D.C. We didn't know he was only fifteen at the time we hired him because he lied to us and said he was eighteen years old.

Vernon was a snotty-nosed kid who was always getting into some type of trouble by either being at the wrong place at the wrong time or talking out of line to the wrong people. He was always costing us money to get him out of trouble, but he was a hell of a guitarist. He was probably one of the best guitarists at the time other than Skip Potts, the wah wah guitar player on "Shaft". Skip was one of the best in the country, especially between 1970 and 1975.

We recorded several albums between 1970 and 1975 at Stax Records, which included "Black Rock" in 1970, "Do You See What I See" in 1971, and "Coldblooded" in 1973, all of which were totally different in many ways, mostly because there was a constant feud and disagreement between the band and Allen when it came down to the musical direction of the band, the song selections for the albums, and practically everything about the band. Allen didn't trust us, or believe in us, enough to let us write much of the early material. It came mostly from the Stax staff writers or by way of songs solicited to us from songwriters outside of Stax. On the other hand, we had not proven to Allen, or ourselves, that we had hit songwriting potential.

We tolerated Allen's controlling attitude—some better than others. Allen was a songwriter himself, so he knew a hit song when he heard it, but I think we trusted him way too much and too often. His controlling nature began wearing heavily on the band. He pushed us way too hard at times, which stopped him from getting the best performance musically and vocally from us. He was often verbally abusive and our self-esteem was often low because he never seemed to be satisfied with our efforts or performances.

As a producer, Allen had a bad habit of making and encouraging the band to write and sound like whomever was hot on the radio or popular at the time. It was okay at first, but as the band got older and started to want an identity of its own, it was a real sore spot for all of us. We began to hate the fact that we were copying other artists and not getting hits from it, but once again, Allen blamed us.

As a singer during those years, I was obsessed with Sly Stone, Ray Charles, and Billy Preston but I was vocally emulating them way too much on records, especially on the "Cold Blooded" album. There were a few cuts on that album that sounded so much like Sly and the Family Stone until it was shameful.

Lucky for us, our live stage show was so powerful and we dressed so differently from any other band (with the exception of Sly and the Family Stone) that even without the hit records, we were gaining popularity all across the country. As a singer, I started being compared to Mick Jagger, Joe Cocker, Tina Turner, and Sly Stone all in one.

Other bands started to take notice of the funky, soul, rock band called The Bar-Kays, especially after the "Black Rock" album. To this day, there are many guys in the industry who say from a production and performance standpoint, "Black Rock" was way ahead of its time,

With our mounting success, the band was elated when Jessie Jackson, former head of the PUSH movement, asked us if we would be interested in writing a theme song for PUSH, a powerful Civil Rights Movement Conference. Jessie had seen the band perform numerous times and was a huge fan.

We accepted Jessie's challenge and came up with a great song entitled "P.U.S.H.", (People United to Save Humanity). We released the song on the "Do You See What I See" album, and performed it live in Chicago at the Operation PUSH Convention. The crowd went crazy.

It was a real honor for us to have made a huge contribution to such a worthy and relevant cause. It made Jet Magazine, a real big deal at the time.

10

Wild 'n Out

In 1974, rumors started circulating around the Stax Studio and offices that the company was in deep debt because of IRS and bank loan problems. There was a possibility that Stax would have to close.

As a band, we were already suffering financially. When I joined the band, I was making $75 a week and that was after I had been in the band a while. It got up to maybe $100 a week, if I recall correctly. That was nowhere near enough for a guy to take care of a family. Remember, I joined The Bar-Kays in March of 1970 and married Marie in August of 1970. Precious was born September of 1971. We were a family living off of next to nothing. Marie had a job, but it didn't pay much either.

The band was getting nervous about what to do with our contract, which for some strange reason, the company didn't want to talk to us about. The other bigger and more popular artists were leaving Stax one by one.

When Stax couldn't pay Isaac Hayes royalties for "Shaft" they compensated him by appointing him Vice-President of Stax. This would keep him from suing the company. Isaac welcomed the title and position because of the kind of person he was—he craved attention.

To Stax Records, The Bar-Kays were just a bunch of wild and crazy musicians who hadn't quite found their niche in the business, but they didn't want to release us from our contract. This was a big problem for us.

As a company play, to keep the band quiet for a while, one day James was called outside to the Stax lot and given the keys to a brand new Mark IV Lincoln Continental. Trust me, they had underlying motives in this gift. James, of course, was surprised and actually he deserved it for the perseverance he had shown throughout the years in reforming the band after the crash, and by adding me as a singer, thereby giving the band new direction.

Little did we know, but the "Coldblooded" album would be the last album that The Bar-Kays would record on the Stax label.

We left behind a lot of completed masters at Stax before it closed. One cut, in particular was called "Holy Ghost", which from the title and lyrics was quite a controversial song. *(Your love, it's got the Holy Ghost, and I feel like I've been born a second time...)*

"Holy Ghost" is by far one of the funkiest tracks and one of my best vocal performances ever. We recorded the song in 1975, but we were afraid to release it because of the subject matter and how it equated physical love with spiritual love and God.

The Gospel community got wind of the song and this gave us even more reservation about releasing it or putting it on any albums.

Among the many stage antics we used in our live show, I started using snakes, which I alone would handle.

I started using the snake one night at a performance in a club in Nashville, Tennessee. The snake was my personal pet. I used to keep it on the bus in a glass cage and watch him eat rats and trip out on it.

One night, the snake's cage was in the wing on stage and I thought it would be a fun idea to bring the snake out on a number. I did it and the crowd went nuts. To think about it, Alice Cooper was the only other artist who personally used snakes in his act. After that night, I started using the snake in every show, introducing it into our act during the last five to ten minutes of our performance. Instantly, it became worldwide news. It elevated the band's presence one hundred percent. I was in every magazine you could name.

Allen and our manager at the time, a lady by the name of Sandy Newman, were all for the snake act. Anything that would bring the band publicity was a good thing.

Allen was never quite comfortable managing the band. He just wanted to stay close to the music and remain the idol maker and control the image of each one of us in the band. He did a very good job of that.

Sandy was a Jewish lady, a fast-talking, sharp, slick, California girl. She knew the business pretty well. For the most part, she and Allen got along. I guess it didn't hurt that both of them were gay, which we all later found out. They were both very respectful of the band and kept their business to themselves.

For the first few years, I used several snakes (Burmese pythons), and named all of them Cecil. The band members were terrified of them. As a precaution, I had one of the roadies keep a long machete knife with instructions that during any performance, and if at any time I got in trouble where the snake tightened around my neck or body and wouldn't ease up, the roadie had instructions to come out and immediately cut the snake's head off so that it would release its hold on me. Otherwise, I could be killed in a matter of minutes. I never used a snake under five feet long. They were terribly strong, so if a snake tightened around my neck I would only have a few minutes to get him off and the only way would be by killing it.

On one occasion, when we had a performance in Memphis, we invited the TV media to come out to the venue and film the rehearsal. I let the snake out so they could film it, and the cameraman accidentally stepped on it and broke its neck. I had to get another snake for that night's performance. I found one at a local pet shop that was about seven feet long. I began singing "Very Superstitious" by Stevie Wonder and immediately the snake coiled around my neck about four times and had his head directly in front of my face for the entire song. It was the only time I was scared to death because I thought the snake was going to bite me in the face. It did not, but after the song was over, I ran to the wing and the roadie uncoiled him from around my neck.

Every show brought new amazement when they would see me stick the snake's head in my mouth or pretend to throw the snake into the front row of the audience. I watched the audience scream, run, and leave the front row seats until they realized I was only pretending to throw the snake.

11
Takeover

In 1975, the IRS finally moved in on Stax and Union Planters Bank called in its loans. Stax closed its doors for good. The IRS came in and padlocked the doors.

Al Bell tried everything he knew to keep the doors open, including convincing the entire staff to work for a year without salary. He was persuasive like that. He had a charming, breathtaking, and somewhat overpowering personality. He could talk an Eskimo out of his coat at the North Pole!

The Bar-Kays and the Staple Singers were the last artists to leave the label. We were devastated, scared, and unsure of our next move.

Allen and the band had a serious meeting after the closing of Stax. He gave us two options, One, break-up the band and go our separate ways or two, pick up our boot straps, get closer to each other, find a place to pay for a year or so, and start writing songs to prepare for shopping for a new record deal. We took all of his advice.

At this time, the band members consisted of me as lead vocalist, James on bass guitar, Winston remained on keyboards, Harvey on sax, Frank Thompson on trombone, Charles "Scoop" Allen on trumpet, and Michael Beard on drums. We released Vernon Burch on lead guitar and hired a guitar player from Philadelphia by the name of Lloyd Smith. There were some other drummers and guitar players who tried out in the interim but this is who we ended up keeping. It was a hot band.

At Allen's request, we took a gig at a hole-in-the-wall club in Memphis called The Family Affair. We played there four nights a week for over a year for next to nothing as pay, but it saved the band and we became incredibly tight. During this yearlong stay, we rented a rehearsal place in midtown and began to write songs to shop. We wrote "Shake Your Rump to the Funk", Too Hot to Stop", "Summer of Our Love", and "Spellbound".

Allen and James ran the band and took care of the band's business during these years, which was cool. James was always a record guy who never forgot a face or a name, an attribute and talent that he still possesses at 66 years of age and one that helps to make him one of the most respected guys in the record industry.

Allen was an introvert. He never took pictures, never wanted to be out front, and never wanted credit for anything publicly. Privately, among us, he reminded us of how much experience he had with writing and producing. He had some huge songs like "Hard to Handle" which had been recorded by Otis Redding and Tom Jones and a host of other Rock 'n Roll artists.

Allen and the band were continuing to work on helping to recreate my image. I worked on finding a vocal style of my own. I knew I didn't have the best voice but I also knew neither did Sly Stone; we were both stylists. I had a distinct style. When you heard my voice on the radio, you knew it was me.

James found an attorney in Memphis by the name of Jim Zumwalt. He was not experienced as a music attorney but low hanging first for us since we couldn't really afford the best music attorney representation for the band.

James had started dialogue with Mercury Records and had started to shop the songs we had written. He had gotten a good bite, especially on "Shake Your Rump to the Funk". We took a chance and let Jim handle the deal.

Between Mercury loving the music they heard and Jim doing a pretty good job at negotiating, he landed us a deal at Mercury with a $500,000 signing bonus. God surely looked down on all of this because it was the very first recording deal Jim had ever done in his career.

To this day, Jim still tells this story to his clients and friends and brags how The Bar-Kays gave him his start in the music industry. Jim went on to open his own firm. Today, he is probably one of the top ten music attorneys in the country with more connections than ninety percent of all music attorneys in the business. He is on a first name basis with ninety percent of all of the record label presidents in the business. By the way, we did that deal over lunch, a total of one hour. *And the band plays on.*

12

Too Hot to Stop

Our first album for Mercury was called "Too Hot to Stop". Though it sold well it fell short of gold, but as time went on it surpassed gold status in sales. Allen produced the album. This album didn't take quite as long as some of the previous ones. There were some albums that we would take almost a year to record, finish, only to then have Allen scrap the entire project and make us start all over again from scratch. After that, he would often take us to a totally new city and studio, most of the time it was wherever Sly Stone was recording. He said it was for motivation. It was totally crazy when it came to recording. We would work sometimes for two or three days on song recordings, then twenty or thirty hours without sleep. Allen would record us in shifts.

Our record deal called for one album a year and Jim Zumwalt had also made a great publishing deal that gave us $20,000 cash on each album we turned in so life was getting better for Larry Dodson and The Bar-Kays.

We somehow talked Michael Toles' ex-wife into posing nude for our album cover. It was so funny because she wouldn't agree to do the front cover but she did agree to do the back cover nude with a wig. We had to use smoke around her so Michael would never know it was her, and it worked.

The Bar-Kays shared our new record label home with label mates like the Ohio Players, Kool and the Gang, The Gap Band, and other chart topping hot artists. Our stock was going up.

The catalogue that Stax once owned was changing ownership. Fantasy Records finally ended up buying a bulk of the recorded masters from Union Planters Bank, which had taken ownership of them for debts owed them by Stax. Among those masters was a finished version of "Holy Ghost" and a second version of the same song we recorded called "Holy Ghost Reborn", which was not nearly as good as the original version.

Meanwhile, we were getting settled into our new label home and had recorded and turned in our second album on the label called "Flying High On Your Love". It was our first gold album on the label. Two of our most popular songs were recorded on this album, "Let's Have Some Fun" and "Attitude".

There is a rather funny story behind recording "Attitude". We wrote the song but we only had two verses to it and no bridge. We often recorded the demos of our songs live and I would do a rough vocal to help the band's vibe. Well, we did this demo and recorded it all with just the two verses and then went upstairs to take a listen.

Allen listened to us play it back a couple of times and then said, "That's it. I don't want you guys to do anything else to the song."

I said, "Well, what about the fact that the song only has two verses and no bridge or structure?"

Allen said, "You guys really captured some magic on this one."

The only thing we added to the record was to bring our main roadie into the studio. He put a squeaking bird sound on a few spots. The crazy part about it is that no one mentioned how short the song was with the exception of a few DJ's who found it peculiar. To this day, "Attitude" remains one of our most requested and popular ballads.

It was becoming quite obvious that the cornerstone of The Bar-Kays' future was centered around me, Larry Dodson, both on record and live performances. Our live stage show was becoming more elaborate and entertaining with each album.

We rehearsed constantly and put a lot of time and attention on our stage outfits. We had two top 10 singles from the "Too Hot to Stop" album and two top 20 singles from the "Flying High on Your Love" album.

To keep up with Allen and his demanding and unbelievable recording schedules, some of us in the band started using drugs. Some of us started using cocaine, but we couldn't afford much, so it never became too much of a problem, at least not then. We learned later that Allen was dropping pills to stay awake.

13

Holy Ghost

In December 1978, Fantasy Records released "Holy Ghost" from the album called "Money Talks", and it went through the roof. It broke in New Orleans and D.C. and the song never looked back.

"Holy Ghost" busted the top 10 R&B charts and peeked at number 9 after being on the charts for 17 weeks. Fantasy had been holding the song to release at just the right time, which proved to be an incredibly smart move that worked.

Meanwhile, over at Mercury Records, we had turned in a smash single called "Shine", which was an Earth, Wind & Fire rip-off, but during those years all of the self-contained bands copied a little from each other. I remember when we were in the studio recording "Too Hot to Stop", and guess what, The Commodores were in the same studio recording "Too Hot to Trot". We were friends but they never let us come into their sessions...Umm, I wondered why.

The Bar-Kays certainly had their share of rip-offs. This concerned Allen. Allen was a master at dissecting a current hit record and having us to get as close as we could to reaching the *it factor* of the song and trust that my distinct vocals would make the difference. Most of the time it worked, but the band hated the whole rip-off concept to get a hit.

By 1978, we were three albums deep at Mercury Records. The "Light of Life" album released and only had one strong single, which was "Shine". "Shine" turned out to be a smash and saved the album from being a weaker Bar-Kays album. We released it a few months after "Holy Ghost" and it soared to number 14 on the R&B charts. Now we had two hit records out at the same time. It was an exciting twelve months for us.

We made a lot of money on the concert side but Allen had everyone on a salary year round so there were no royalties, no lump sums, just a year round salary. What's wrong with this picture?

"Holy Ghost" had gotten so hot in D.C. that we would play there three or four times a year for good money. At one time, it was one of the most sampled records ever recorded.

Up to this point, the writing team consisted of me, Winston, and Harvey. Winston did all of the tracking. Harvey and I did the lyrics and melodies. Band member, Mark Bynum and I did a lot of the background vocals.

We came to the studio everyday and spent eight to ten hours working on songs for the band. Allen started this process with us early in the band and it became a habit. As we started to come up with hits, he slowly gave us more leeway and accepted more of the songs that we submitted. James was the record guy and talked to the label a lot, along with Jim Zumwalt who was now our permanent attorney.

Allen started getting us into a lot of trouble with the label by not turning our albums in on time. In typical Allen fashion, he was never satisfied with our performances or his performance as a producer. The label would fine us, suspend us, or do whatever it took to get us to turn our albums in on time.

We were so late on the "Flying High" album and when we thought we were done with it, we realized we were a song short. The label gave us an ultimatum to get it completed and turn it in or this time we were done. Jim used every trick he knew to buy us time so there we were, in Ardent Studios in Memphis, with three studios recording or mixing cuts. We turned one side over to the mastering guy, Larry Nix, to master one side while we were writing and recording the last cut that we made up on the floor. We cut it live with no drums because there were none in the studio available, and we had no written lyrics.

After almost two hours of being on the floor with tambourines and all the guys around two microphones, we cut a song called "Give It Up". We recorded and mixed it at the same time with William Brown, then our regular engineer. We rushed the song down the hall to mastering and Larry Nix mastered the other side of the album. We stayed up all night in the studio and rushed the album to Chicago the next day, hand-delivered by James. It was the messiest shit we had ever done. I was so embarrassed 'til I couldn't hold my head up. It just wasn't a good album. Thank God for "Shine".

Cocaine use was beginning to be somewhat of a problem that no one would admit. Now that we were on the road and doing more concerts, we had people giving and selling drugs to us. It was a time bomb waiting to explode in the band. We did a pretty good job of hiding it from Allen at first but soon he started to see the drug dealer come around us and began to get suspicious. He hated drugs.

The only thing Allen hated as much as the drugs were the women in our lives. With our huge signing bonus of $500,000, Jim Zumwalt got his attorney fees plus each one of the band members got a $10,000 bonus. That would go on record as being the only time in the band's professional existence, while Allen was alive, that we got a lump sum of money like that.

We had a meeting and agreed to buy a tour bus. That was one of the few logical expenditures the band agreed to make. Later, Allen talked us into buying a studio, saying it would be a good investment. Allen had this vision of us becoming a full production company where we would sign, produce, and record acts. However, the band was more interested in staying on the road, having sex, doing drugs, and living rock 'n roll style. We loved the life.

We trusted Allen and Jim. Like most dumb musicians, we didn't pay nearly enough attention to where the money was going. Even James, as the bandleader, didn't keep his eye on the prize close enough and he was smarter than all of us put together.

The band made a decision to elect Winston to be the CFO/Treasurer. Winston has always been honest throughout the band's entire career, but because no one ever challenged Allen or him about expenses, things went uncontested and it seemed we were always short of money to do what we wanted to do.

In the past, we had been getting our outfits made locally by a lady by the name of Laura Johnson and a few other local seamstresses and tailors, but now that we could afford better stuff, we started using designers that designed for The Commodores, Elton John, Sly Stone, The Temptations and other well-known artists. We were paying as much as $30,000 a wop to outfit the band!

14

Keeping a Watchful Eye

Our road manager was a guy by the name of R.L. Jones. He was an amazing man, friend, father figure, and big brother all wrapped up in one. He guided us around, and through, our early years in the band. When Allen was too tough on us, R.L. was the guy who had the courage to go to him, curse him out, if needed, and state our case. R. L. would, could, and did always say those things to Allen that we were too afraid to say. Very often, Allen would take his advice and see our side of a particular point. R.L. drove the tour bus for us until he became ill and could not do it anymore.

Most of the guys, including me, were quite young when we joined the band, and R.L. got us through a lot of tough times. Sometimes when we were on the road with no money to buy food or gas for the bus, R.L. would pull the bus over and get three hotel rooms for the entire band and roadies. We would eat bologna sandwiches and drink Kool-Aid. Then all of us would pile up in those double beds and on the floor after helping R.L. down a fifth or quart of rum and coke. He would get us laughing about something to lift our spirits and make us forget for a moment that we didn't know how we were going to get to the next city to perform.

R. L. always came through for us. I have known him to take his house note and loan it to The Bar-Kays and then slip it back before his wife found out.

There was this one time we were on our way to LA from Memphis to perform at the club Whiskey A Go-Go and the bus broke down in Diming, New Mexico. We had no money and it was over one hundred degrees both day and night. It was going to take $5,000 to fix the motor because it had locked up. R.L. fed us bologna and crackers for five days and made us set up our speaker and PA system on the black top. We rehearsed the show in our shorts until the wrecker came to tow the bus to the repair shop.

R.L. was also the one who helped the guys get through private affairs on the road, especially the ones that involved older females.

Singing artist, Carla Thomas, had a huge crush on Michael Toles. She was doing all she could to get him in bed. R. L. stopped it. Then there was the time when Mary Wilson of the Supremes was head over heels crazy about then fifteen-year old Vernon, our guitarist. Again, R.L. made sure Vernon stayed out of trouble. R.L. would get the guys through these kinds of things.

There was another time that R.L. came to my rescue. It involved actor, Raymond St. James. St. James kept trying his best to get me out to his home alone under the pretense that he wanted to cast me for a part in a western movie he was producing and filming. Now, this one sent R.L. and Allen running to my room every day and night to make sure that I hadn't given in or gone to his ranch to sign off on the deal.

You see, Raymond was a known gay pervert who preyed on young guys and often used this Hollywood line to get the guys out to his home and do who knows what.

Because of the way we dressed and often acted on stage, there were a lot of rumors around Hollywood that me, and several guys in the band, were bisexual. Not unusual at all, and of course, Allen loved the publicity. He was always thinking of things to do or say to attract media attention and create a stink. It was one of the reasons that he pushed the edgy, feminine-styled outfits, especially for me, Harvey, and Winston because we were all rather small in size and could wear anything.

With all of the rumors of me being gay floating around, my hairstyle didn't help. I wore it long and straight by way of very expensive human hair extensions being sewn and braided into my own hair. It looked incredibly real. Even when standing next to me, you couldn't tell that they were extensions. It was an expensive process to keep up.

There was one lady in Memphis who could do my extensions on a professional level and her name was Mrs. Caswell. The extensions may have given me a feminine look but the ladies at our performances went wild because it became me with me being so small. My constant and ever-increasing cocaine use kept my weight off.

I never cared for marijuana. Weed made me paranoid, sleepy, and it was horrible for my voice. I tried performing while high on weed maybe twice. I had such a hard time remembering the words to songs and often where I was, so I never did it again.

Doing a few lines of cocaine before going on stage, however, had just the opposite effect. It made me sharper on stage, more alert, my voice was clearer and I had so much more energy. However, too much cocaine before going on was a nightmare. Like weed, it made me paranoid. My throat would close up about halfway through the show and I would freak out. I had to watch that and be careful not to overdo it before going on stage.

We could always depend on R.L. to tell us the absolute truth about our nightly performances. I don't ever remember him saying the band was fantastic too many times; he just didn't give out those kinds of compliments to the band for some strange reason.

R.L. also reported to Allen regularly about what was going on with the group while we were on the road because Allen was afraid to fly; he was also afraid to travel on the bus at night. He eventually started to come out more when we started headlining dates and co-starring with big artists. We were really starting to kick ass on the live shows. No band wanted to come on behind us or let us on their tour for fear we would steal their glory.

15
InJoy

Winston, Harvey, and I continued to write and grind away as always. Our hard work paid off with one of the best albums we had written and recorded up to this point. It was appropriately titled, "Injoy". Allen had given us a little more freedom to experiment on this album and we did. As far as the label was concerned, we needed to come correct on this album because The Ohio Players, our biggest rivals at the label, were turning in hit album after hit album with at least three number one singles on every album. Even with their bad attitudes and looking down on the other artists on the label, and huge cocaine problems in their band, they were phenomenal in the studio. They left little to be desired on their live performances. All in all they changed the way R&B and Pop radio played and approached black music at that time.

Satch, the leader of The Ohio Players, got so cocky at one point that he invited me, James, and a select few members of the band to his home in Dayton, Ohio. He had bowls of cocaine in the rooms where people were mingling. He invited me and James to another room to personally talk. There was an ashtray full of cocaine in there. He tried to convince me and James to sign The Bar-Kays to his own label. In a nutshell, this meant he would get our recording budget and control our publishing deal. We would be working for him. We had no idea he was going to talk about something as farfetched as us signing to his production company. Of course, we said no but we did get high that night and stashed quite a bit of his cocaine before leaving early the next morning. Satch never brought the subject up again for as long as we knew him.

The Ohio Players continued to make incredible records for years to come at Mercury and Polygram Records with the very distinct voice of lead singer, Sugarfoot, at the microphone.

Allen was infatuated with The Ohio Players, their records, their success, and their ability to capture the magic on tape time and time again. He made us copy a lot of their style, musically. Since Sugarfoot and I had a lot in common, vocally, as singers, both of us being stylist singers rather than crooners, it wasn't hard for me to imitate Sugarfoot with his familiar *ah* and my *well* that I used on practically every record I recorded, as well as the *ow*, which I borrowed from Sugarfoot. And guess what, so did Maurice White from Earth, Wind & Fire, Larry Blackman from Cameo, Mike Cooper from Confunkshun, and later on Sugarbear from the EU Band with their big hit, "The Butt." Like me, Sugarfoot's voice was so distinct that everyone knew he would be almost impossible to replace if that ever had to happen.

Nevertheless, we struck gold with the "Injoy" album. As writers, we put everyone's name on the record as writers but it was not true. Allen asked us to do this so that the money would be shared equal, with the hopes that money would not become an issue that might lead to us breaking up. Many groups often suffered from money issues that led to break up.

Allen's suggestion sounded like a good idea at first, but as time went on, it only proved to make the band lazy. It totally destroyed the initiative that some of the guys may have had to write and help us out on the writing side. I mean, if you were going to have the same royalty split as the guy who was really spending the time writing the songs, why write and contribute?

The danger became evident when those who had nothing to do with writing the hits suddenly became experts on what was good and what was not good, just to have something to say. It was often offensive to the three of us and we had to live with the arrangement that was in effect concerning the royalty split. To us, only Allen had the right to give us meaningful criticism and constructive criticism on our work. Not that we didn't listen to all of the guys, but it got to a point that most of the guys only came around to collect and cash their weekly checks.

Allen was smart and to offset the potential and growing problem, he would privately bail us out of personal problems, there was this one time Harvey needed a down payment on a new home and I needed to catch up my mortgage with four or five grand. He immediately came to our rescue to keep us cool. We understood that he would not go quite that far with the nonproductive, nonparticipants in the band.

During the writing stages, I had the idea to write a song that would be led by someone in the band other than me, which could have only been Mark or Sherman who had a decent falsetto voice. We wrote a song, which Sherman led, called "Running In and Out of my Life". It took him a while to record the song because it was his first rodeo singing lead on a song and the key was very high. We ended up with the best performance that we could get out of Sherman and the song stayed on the album to help sell the album.

The best song on the album was the first single called "Move Your Boogie Body", which rose to #7 on the R&B charts after about 18 weeks on the chart. It was released in October of 1979 followed by one of the biggest Pop records we ever had called "Today Is the Day", which we released February 1980. It was dangerously close to the Commodore's hit record "Easy" but again Winston, Harvey, and I followed orders from Allen, which was for us to bring a track similar to whatever was the hottest song out at the time. Our orders were to lyrically and melodically make it happen and depend on my distinct voice to make the difference.

"Injoy" went gold fast and that album cover, in my opinion, was the best group photo we had ever taken. Up to this point, believe it or not, there were only one or two pictures floating around of Allen. He didn't believe in taking pictures and there was no such thing as the internet so the public never knew what Allen looked like. Well, on this photo session, there was a shot that Fred Toma, the photographer, caught of Allen fixing one of the jackets or something. We used that shot as the photo on the sleeve cover with

Allen not knowing because he wouldn't approve. That was the only picture he ever had on any Bar-Kays' album cover.

We were constantly recording tracks for the next album, writing the songs for the next album, or on the road performing the hits from the album. There was little time for family life, which wasn't good for any of us. Although we were extremely hot and popular, our bank accounts did not reflect it. Those of us who were married with families felt it the most. When Marie asked me about where all the money was going all I could say was we had a lot of overhead operating the studio, two tour buses, the offices, staff, and year round salaries. All of what I told her was true but what was hard for our wives and close female friends to understand was why there was never a lump sum of money given to the band for anything at any time, which led to the next question—is your manager or attorney stealing money from the band? It was becoming the main topic of the back room meetings in the band. The cocaine bills didn't help the situation at all either. The only guys in the band that stayed pretty clean of cocaine were Winston and Harvey.

Mike, the drummer, was a weed head who smoked the very best weed one could ever find right before he went on stage like clockwork. It seemed to make him more alert and play better.

James never needed much rest and was always working on something pertaining to promoting The Bar-Kays. He was smart beyond belief, but the cocaine use got him, too. He was a loner by nature and he never wanted anyone to know exactly what he was doing or why he was doing it.

As time passed, he became the cocaine dealer in the band. In fact, much to our surprise he became one of the biggest dealers in the city. He would later get busted and go to jail after being set-up on a drug deal in one of the local restaurants. He ended up going before a harsh judge and even as popular as we were, our money and might couldn't keep him from going to jail. Luckily, he only had to do about four months.

After being released from jail, James married a young lady who was the office secretary. I'm not quite sure, but I think that was his second marriage. He would go on to marry two more times.

16
As One

We went on to record the "As One" album which I do believe we fought Allen over every cut. We were constantly trying to be more original as a band and Allen wanted us to appear to be on a spiritual mission of some sort, but thank God for Winston coming up with the hot track for a cut we called "Boogie Bodyland", which landed us a #7 spot on the R&B charts. We also did an inspirational tune titled "Deliver Us", which was inspired by The Commodore's cut that they had out at the time.

It's really funny when I look back and think about groups like Earth, Wind & Fire who used to open for us at concerts. Some of the groups that got their first start on the concert circuit were groups like New Edition and Switch whose first concert gig was opening for The Bar-Kays, Lakeside, and The Commodores.

There was a time early in our career when Earth, Wind & Fire and The Bar-Kays were playing a college somewhere in the south. At that time, we carried our own P.A. system which consisted of eight Shure columns and lights that our roadie who we called "Car Tire", built for us.

Verdine White of Earth, Wind & Fire asked Car Tire if they could use our sound and lights. Car Tire remarked very smartly to them, "'Hell, no.'" At the time we knew nothing about this confrontation because we were at the hotel. Verdine and Maurice swore that they would never play with us again. To this day, they never have and they continue to talk about that incident. Wow! Talk about being cursed with memory.

In 1981, we struck gold again with a killer concept album called "Night Cruising". Allen got the idea from Rick James' "Street Songs" album, and put us on a mission to write as many songs as we could about nightlife. The writing team went to work.

We had a lot of fun with this album because it had a lot to do with the kind of life we were living on the road, on and off the stage. Of course, we fought hard not to make the album cover similar to Rick's but we lost that battle.

We wrote hits on the "Night Cruising" album like "Hit and Run" which peaked at #5, "Traffic Jammer", "Unforgettable Dream", which is still one of our most requested and popular ballads, and the west coast anthem, "Freaky Behavior" which we totally ripped off Rick James' "Super Freak." We popped gold again and by this time we had three certified gold albums at Polygram Records. Our calendar filled up fast with tour dates behind this album.

Being a lead singer had its perks. I was getting to know all of the heavy weights like Rick James and Charlie Wilson, to name a few. Rick and I would go on to become very good friends. He was crazy about Marie. He would never admit getting a big part of his look from watching me early in my career, but if you put a picture of me and him side by side, you would plainly see where his image got its help from.

Whenever Rick came into town or I would go to see him after a concert, he would always give me carte blanche. He treated me with respect. Even when we got high together, we would talk about sensible stuff, not a bunch of cocaine foolishness.

Rick was always concerned about me and I about him. I think he saw so much of himself (the destructive part) in me. He would always check to see if I was financially okay. I remember once when he came to town, we were in the hotel room and he asked me if I still had my house. I told him that I did not. Before I could give him an explanation, he became real angry because he already knew what had happened, and he was right. I had let the cocaine get in the way and my house note had gotten nine months behind. I'll never forget how ashamed I felt. Without saying another word, the look on his face said, "'I'm Rick James and I can afford whatever I'm doing and you're Larry Dodson and you can't and don't you ever forget that and never let your family down again.'" He was absolutely right.

The 80's were proving to be the best and most productive years The Bar-Kays had experienced up to this point in our career, but as a band, we were slowly dividing in our allegiance.

James, still our bandleader, had his ideas about how things should be handled, such as the concerts, friends, record royalties, and expenditures with the band's money, especially the small salaries we were getting. Most of the band, including myself, would side with Allen, even though we agreed with James. We were just too afraid of Allen to go against him. This led to a huge problem with the friendships in the band.

In spite of the differences like cocaine abuse that was now going on with almost all of the guys, we were really scared for Charles' "Scoop" ever-growing use of angel dust, a terrible substance that is laced with marijuana. Angel dust can eventually drive anyone who smokes it more than a few times out of their mind, literally. Charles was starting to look, talk, and act real strange. It was really sad. Musically, he still managed to play okay but the constant use of angel dust would later cause us to force him to take a leave of absence to get help. We eventually got him to stop and things got back to almost normal.

In spite of all of the hindrances, our next two albums, "Proposition" in 1982 and "Dangerous" in 1984 went gold and produced top 10 singles and hits like "Anticipation", "She Talks To Me With Her Body", "Do It Let Me See You Shake", "Sexomatic", and our biggest single ever, "Freakshow on the Dance Floor." "Freakshow" peaked at #2. It was our first real video directed by a pretty cool guy by the name of Marcus Pinison.

With five gold albums under our belt, we could do no wrong at the record label. We pretty much got what we wanted, and Allen was always asking the label for money for one thing or another. The record company didn't care much for him.

The only reason we could not get a No.1 single was because we released our album around the same time as Michael Jackson. Our singles would be out at the same time as Michael Jackson's and our chances for No.1 went downhill. Michael Jackson would be No.1 and we could never knock him off that spot. To this day, we have never had a number one record.

The band soared to new heights with my distinct vocals. The band's funky tracks made it easy for me. Our signature was Winston's synth keyboard lead lines, the moog and bass lines combined, and those simple but distinct horn lines in most of the songs. We arranged for real strings and used other horn players on some albums when our guys couldn't cut it or if we wanted something really romantic in the ballads. We started using the drum machine more as well as the synth horns mixed in with the real ones. It was just a way of changing with the times and staying ahead of the game and the other artists. We did the same thing with our dress on stage and our hairstyles.

When we dyed our hair so would the rest of the country. They looked to The Bar-Kays for the next fashion trend ideas and we loved it. You could usually look at us on our album covers and get a hint as to where we were headed with fashion, at least for the next year.

"Freakshow" ended up being placed in a hit movie called "Breakin" and the sound track album went platinum! It seemed that we could do no wrong. The "Freakshow" video was great and was a terrific visual for the band.

We performed on *Don Kirsner's Rock Concert*, a Pop show that was very hard for black acts to get asked to do back then. We did *Soul Train* about three times, with very elaborate fashion outfits from Elton John's design.

We were headlining big concerts, (we were going to Asia but never to Europe for some reason), getting

$25,000 to $35,000 a night, excellent money in those days but, internally, the fight between Allen, James, and the rest of the band was getting worse because we were too chicken shit to take sides with James and fight Allen.

I had a nice home. James had a nice home, and Winston lived with Allen in an elite neighborhood in a swank bachelor pad with a swimming pool and a Mercedes. The other guys had apartments with their girlfriends, but Lloyd, the guitar player, lived in the ghetto like a bum.

Shortly after we got our first and only royalty split, Allen took us all to the Cadillac dealership and leased a Cadillac for me, one for Mike, one for Winston, and one for Scoop. James leased a Mercedes. Harvey and Lloyd got something else. The bills were paid from the kitty, one of the few things done like that.

The label started releasing "Best Of" albums on the band and they did well. James saw it was a losing battle fighting Allen and the band so in 1986, after being in The Bar-Kays more than 20 years, James decided to leave. At that time, most of our recordings were done at Ardent Studios. So much so, that they built a Studio C room especially for us because we spent so much time recording in Studio B. ZZ Top kept Studio A booked all of the time.

Just before James left the group, things did change. The money was divided equitably and Allen hated it. We actually saw more and could account for more of the money.

As I said, Allen loved to record and he had a lot of bad habits. He smoked almost four packs of cigarettes a day and drank probably 10-15 cups of coffee a day which consumed a five-pound bag of sugar a week. He had already suffered one mild heart attack at the studio from these bad habits. Little did we know that John Frye, the studio owner, had taken a quarter of a million dollar insurance policy out on Allen when he agreed to build the new room for The Bar-Kays. He knew Allen wouldn't live long with habits like he had and working himself like he did.

When James left the band he moved to Houston to start a promotion business. He and Allen never spoke again. *And the band plays on.*

17

Life Goes On

In 1987, while on the telephone talking to Winston and Harvey, Allen had a massive heart attack and ultimately died.

Allen's death was no surprise to me. He had once or twice talked about the fact that he wasn't going to have a long life. He was an atheist and often got upset with us because of our belief and trust in God.

Personally, I think deep down in his heart, he believed in God, but was just afraid to admit it. He was gay and that went against God's teaching. That's just my opinion. He and I were very close and he never approached me or got out of line with me with his lifestyle. I respected him for not imposing.

Allen always enjoyed the rumors surrounding the band because it made the band more popular. His whole life surrounded us, The Bar-Kays.

R.L., our road manager, was Allen's only friend other than a few songwriters like Henderson Thigpen and James Banks who were the co-writers on "Holy Ghost."

As I grew older and started producing other artists, I found myself somewhat emulating Allen and his producing approaches. I learned so much from him but I didn't appreciate it until I was older and wiser. I really missed him, and with James no longer a part of the band, his presence was missed, too. Two of my best friends were gone out of my life.

James was a proud guy. He stayed away from the band and got lost in the promotion of the record world, his main love. I really do believe if he had his way he would have chosen to be a record label president; he would have been good at it because he was a sponge. He soaked up all of the knowledge he could from all of the record CEO's and record Execs, as well as all of the old time promotion guys, and they loved him.

When James was with The Bar-Kays, he and I were roommates on the road. I watched him grow from a bass player to a very good and smart promotion man. His knowledge would soon pay off for both of us in the years to come.

After James left, Harvey, Winston, Lloyd and I continued the band. The parting members each sold their publishing rights before leaving for a small sum, giving ownership of the publishing to me, James, Harvey and Winston. It was a horrible move on their parts but they all needed money and they were so bitter at the time they left the band, as most guys were when they quit or got fired.

One of the best drummers we had was Alvin Hunter who was the drummer on the *Wattstax* movie and soundtrack. He died of a drug overdose in

Memphis after being fired from the band for his drug use and bad temper. Alvin and Allen stayed into it; Alvin had a problem with authority.

Another excellent drummer was Willie Hall, who played on all of Isaac Hayes' albums, including "Shaft" and played in Isaac's road band. He also had a huge drug problem and never got along with Allen and did not agree with how Allen controlled the band.

As far as a musician, I consider Ben Cauley to be by far one of the best trumpet players ever. I never heard anyone play the trumpet in high registers before Ben and few since Ben. With his sharp dress, he was the ladies' man of the group, often taking on three or four women a night when we were on the road in the early years.

One night in LA, we all decided we would try to smoke some angel dust, including Ben. Ben never got high and didn't drink. He took a couple of tokes and went outside to jump over the banister of the hotel where we were staying. We grabbed him, and that's the only reason he didn't kill himself.

Meanwhile, we had a gig the next night at the world renowned PJ's. Actor Desi Arnaz was in the audience that night, along with famous guitarist Wah Wah Watson, and some of The Temptations. We were all high and paranoid. We were all in different keys and looking at each other as if it was the other guy's fault. We sounded horrible and couldn't wait until the set was over. After that, we never smoked angel dust again. I have never touched it again in my life; it is a terrible drug with horrible side effects.

We continued the band without James and Allen. The record deal was fine. The label quickly got over James being gone and as long as I was there and the writing team, Harvey, Winston, and me continued to write hits, everything was cool.

The last album we recorded together before James left and Allen died was "Banging the Walls", which was released in 1985. From that album, which was heavily influenced by Allen's favorite artist Prince, came the hit, "Your Place Or Mine". It topped the R&B charts at #12. Not quite making to top 10, but it felt like it. It was so funky and our fans went crazy when we released the remixed version, which was remixed in New York like the remixed version of "Sexomatic". The remix turned the cuts into brand new records and drove the club spectrum insane, something we could never quite get in the studios in Memphis with William Brown, our lifetime engineer or from any of the other sharp "white" engineers at Ardent where our gold and platinum albums had been recorded.

It became obvious to us, and the record label, that those guys in New York had their ears pinned to the pulse of what was going on and what the next best thing was musically so we didn't get in the way, not one time, with our laid back southern ideas. Even our own engineer had to admit the remix from the New York studio was the shit.

Things had been going well for the band before and after James left. We were making the news in all sorts of ways, whether it was for getting busted with drugs or the drug stories with Rick James, Charlie Wilson, and myself hanging out on the road, the wild all-night parties, and being banned out of cities for streaking when that became popular. No black band had the nerve to take off all of their clothes and run around the stage at a performance. The Bar-Kays did it. Not in every city, but certainly in a lot of them until we started to get banned from venues. Then, of course, we had to slow down with that press shit because it was bothering us.

We had broken the attendance record at the Mid-south Coliseum, which had been held by Elvis Presley, and for that we were very proud for a number of reasons. First of all, the hundreds and thousands of Elvis fans could not believe that a black band could outdraw Elvis in Memphis or be more popular than he was. Yet, we were both at times.

Our attendance record ended up getting broken by none other than Al Green. So what do you say but 'hell yeah.' Another brother beat Elvis out and not just another brother but an iconic figure with an incredible voice. Al ended up living right around the corner from me later on, although he had three or four homes in Memphis. One of them was a huge ranch way out in the northern part of town called Shelby Farms. Al was a strange bud. In my opinion, he was bi-polar because he had so many personalities and each of them could sing their ass off.

Up to this point in our career, we had only done two videos, "Freakshow" and "Your Place or Mine." To this day, they are my favorites. Marius Pinsnor produced both. He had my number as well as the band's number for capturing our images. For me, it was the slim, sexy, androgynous, longhaired kid who was a cross between Mick Jagger and Tina Turner, if there was such a thing. However, it made for interesting chatter, press coverage, and talk among the industry and that was all that mattered. The wives hated it, of course, especially the rumors of the band members being gay or bisexual when they knew better.

18

Drugs Takeover

There was a dark period in my career where Larry Dodson, the sane, kind person sort of left the building and in walked this totally different Larry Dodson, a result of my constant drug and alcohol abuse. Snorting coke had quickly gotten way out of control; both for my pocket book and for my physical health. I was down to a little over 100 pounds and starting not to show up for recording sessions, which was not like me at all.

A few years back, on one of our frequent trips to LA, I met a smooth hustler chick who took me over to one of her rich friend's house in Beverly Hills. Somewhere during the evening, we were sitting at the bar having a drink when she pulled out a pipe and a plate with some white looking rocks on it. She asked if I had ever freebased before and I told her no. Freebasing was what it was called then. Today it's called smoking crack. She took a hit and convinced me to take a hit. I don't have to tell you what happened next. I had never in all my years of getting high, ever felt so good. The only catch was freebasing or 'smoking crack' made me want more. Then I would get so high until I became afraid and didn't want anymore. I'm bringing this up now because I started hanging out with folks who smoked crack and didn't snort much anymore. These were people who stayed up all night, every night, and were irresponsible. I became just like them.

I started staying out all night, drinking heavily, and not remembering much of what had happened the night before. Crack was a drug straight from hell, delivered by the devil. Very few people who were addicted to it ever got back to a normal life. Mainly because of the things craving the drug made you do. Unlike heroin, it was not cheap. I had to be banked up to support a crack cocaine addiction. I didn't have a spiritual life at that time and when you're addicted to crack, there is little time for the Lord. Pathetic.

When Allen died, it was in the middle of the "Contagious" album. Counting the "Best Of" album, this was our twelfth album on Mercury. Five of which had gone gold. The record label wanted an outside producer to finish the project. We were all in favor of this idea. By all I mean me, Harvey, and Winston. Lloyd, the guitarist, had left by this time. He wasn't contributing anything but good looks at this point and by the way, at last count, he had about 15 or 16 kids. He was really blessed because none of the crazy moms ever took him to court or busted him out for child support or anything like that. It was truly amazing. He was the kind of guy who never gave us any trouble but musically he just didn't have much to contribute.

Somehow we got talked into letting R.J. of the band, R.J. Latest Arrival, produce a few cuts and help us salvage the album. We had already started it and it didn't have a hit on it at that point. We agreed on a price and I went to Detroit to write and record with R.J. and his band. He produced one hit called "Shackles On Ya Feet", but he was known around the industry as a producer. Me, R.L. and his wife wrote a song called "Certified True." It turned out to be a killer record that rose to #9 on the R&B charts. It was well recorded and was one of my favorite songs for many years.

Meanwhile, my drinking, drugging, and partying continued. Marie and I had to get housekeepers to help with the home, kids, and cooking because we were both having a little too much fun. There was a year and a half of no music, just touring in and out of the country and the band still sounded great.

Musically, things were changing and radio was changing a lot, too. There was this new electronic thing happening that was breaking bands up because it didn't require a lot of guys to make a record anymore.

19

Recording with My Idol

In 1989, Mercury Records asked me, Harvey, and Winston what we thought about bringing in an outside producer to produce a few cuts on us. I continued to be involved in a terrible life style, but we kept the label interested by supplying them with pretty good records, so I thought bringing in an outside producer was a good idea for a couple of reasons. One, I needed to get away from the crowd that I was hanging around and causing me to be non-productive, and two, it wouldn't hurt to have an outside force to help keep us on the charts, especially in the top ten column.

They chose Jerry Goldstein who had been Sly Stone's manager and also the group War's manager. I didn't know much about his producing ability but at this point in our career, our voice didn't matter much; it was more about what the label thought was best for us. Jerry did a couple of cuts on the album, which I ended up writing, and Winston played almost everything as always. James Mtume, percussionist and founder of the funk and soul group Mtume did three cuts on the album (we used two). The album was called "Animal." We later found out it was a backdoor deal closed between friends at the label and they overpaid Mtume greatly. So much so until before starting the project, which he kept putting off, he took his entire family, I mean immediate grandparents, grandkids, cousins, and all to the islands with the money they paid him. This, of course, ate up our budget but they went into a special fund and gave him funds from that account as well. They all split a bundle.

The record label also cut a deal with these two kids from New York. One was an ex keyboard player from Cameo, and the other one was a lesser producer of sorts named Trevor Gale.

Trevor was a nice guy. Me, Trevor, and the other kid got along really well. Throughout all of my drinking, drugging, and partying I managed to stay in good recording voice.

However, my songwriting was in a slump. Yet, somehow we always managed to find that one song that kept us in the top 10 and kept us working, and guess what, now, WE controlled the concert money and divided it up as we saw fit!

Once again, we came up with a strong song called "Struck By You". "Struck By You" made it all the way to #11 on the R&B charts. Sure, I would have liked a #2 or #3 song, but at this point I was alright with this moderate success.

Mtume lived in New Jersey. He wanted to record in New York but he worked slow. He and I hit it off good, and the outside producers respected me. I was easy to get along with. I didn't have the visible drug addict habits like showing up late, in bad voice, or being uninvolved. I was always much involved with the project, no matter who the producer was.

I went to New Jersey alone to begin working. Somewhere in conversation, Mtume mentioned that he had Sly Stone living in a house near him and he was taking care of him and trying to get him to record again. My heart almost stopped beating at the thought of getting to meet Sly, my all-time favorite artist. Mtume said he would arrange a meeting. And of course, I asked him what kind of shape Sly was in. Mtume told me when Sly came to him, he had five dollars to his name. Mtume said he hooked Sly up with his friend named Ruby. Sly liked Ruby and Ruby took care of him. Sly was still getting high and smoking crack. So was Mtume, I later found out.

The day I went to Mtume's house it was around eleven in the morning. Sly was already in the bathroom doing his thing. Mtume and I waited for about an hour and a half. Sly finally came out with no shoes on. He greeted everyone; I was speechless. It didn't matter that he was wasted. Just to be in the same room with him was magical to me. I knew every song he ever recorded and could sing it just like him. He was my dude!

We talked and he told me that maybe we could do something together before the album was done. I could hardly contain my excitement. I was happier than a kid on Christmas morning. After leaving Mtume's house, I asked Mtume what he thought the chances were that Sly would really write with me or maybe do a duet with me. Mtume said he would ask Sly and he did. It didn't happen right then, but it did happen.

Sly and I spent an entire month together in a popular New York studio. We worked on a lot of song ideas. In my entire musical career, the time I spent working with Sly Stone was one of the most precious memories that I have ever had. We spent countless hours talking. He told me incredible stories that he remembered about the concerts, the money, and how it came and went, and his relationship with the record label. What was most fascinating was when he told me about some of his recording tactics and tricks. For instance, when he couldn't get a particular base drum sound on a record, he would use a real basketball, bounce it on the floor, record the sound, and use it for the base drum sound. That was just one of many fascinating stories.

Mtume told me Sly, for more strange reasons, would never go into the vocal booth to record and never really said why. So, I felt truly special when I asked him and convinced him to do a background vocal on a song we wrote together called "Just Like A Teeter Totter". His talent for working lyrics was out of this world, witty, and full of satire at the same time. In my opinion, he said in his songs all the things that we (The Bar-Kays) were much too apprehensive, afraid, or whatever words you want to use for being too chicken shit to say what was on our minds no matter whose toes we stepped on.

Vocally, Sly and I could get so close on record that we couldn't tell whose part was whose when we did background or adlibbed together.

Sometimes Sly would be in an exceptionally good mood and play and sing me songs that never came out or that he was working on for his next album. He was a perfect gentleman, and worked hard in the studio. I can truthfully say that he took a liking to me and nicknamed me "Baby Boy." I think he saw and felt how much I truly admired him. He was flattered at how much I tried to sound like him on records.

Sly and Mtume would often have long private meetings during the sessions. It wasn't any of my business so I kept it that way.

Sly had a book that he always brought with him to the studio. When he went to the bathroom he would often take this book with him. He called this 'going to Oakland.' When he would leave he would say, "I'll be right back, Baby Boy. I'm going to Oakland."

He left the book on the control board one day. I looked inside. The book had a hollow mold inside of it in the shape of a crack pipe. This made everything make sense. When he would say he was 'going to Oakland,' I recalled how crazy he looked when he came out of the bathroom. Now I understood why our sessions were usually pretty much over after he came out of the bathroom—we couldn't get much done when he was high.

During the month I spent with him, Sly never got high in front of me. I totally respect him for that. I know it took a lot of will for him not to get high during our sessions. He also thought enough of what he and I were doing that he stayed sober while we were writing and recording.

I had written a beautiful ballad called "Leaving You." Mtume helped me to tighten it up. We put strings on it and kept it on the "Contagious" album. We ended up using the songs "Leaving You" and "Teeter Totter" for that album.

It took a little longer in New Jersey than it should have. Harvey, Winston, and Marie were worried that being around Sly was exacerbating my cocaine use when Sly had nothing to do with it. If I wanted a little 'package' then Mtume would simply say, "'You wanna know something?'" I would reply, "Yes," and the dope man would come and bring me a motivational package. Mtume was smart and private. I never saw him get high either, but I know that he did!

20
Mending the Gap

With the record label executives constantly changing, Allen dead, James no longer with us to keep us in the loop with the new guys, and Jim Zumwalt not working on our behalf with the label, but most of all our now declining album sales, Mercury dropped The Bar-Kays after the "Animal" album. For the second time, we found ourselves in our career without a record deal.

With James no longer part of the group it was strange between the two of us because we hardly talked. I didn't really know why. I wasn't mad at him, but it was hard for him to forgive us for not standing up to Allen with him.

He was doing well in the promotion business. Being a smart guy, he always landed on his feet no matter what he did or where he was. Eventually, James and I started talking more. Knowing James like I did, I was a little suspicious as to why all of a sudden he was being so nice.

I understood the reason for his change of demeanor when James called me one day and told me that he found some guys who wanted to invest in a tour. He wanted to arrange a meeting between them and us to talk more about it. I didn't mind it on the business side if it was a kickback or something in it for him, but I was concerned about who these guys really were since promoting was not all James did, if you get my drift.

Needless to say, we met with the guys. They booked a tour that had The Bar-Kays as headliners, Levert who was riding on a #1 high with his song "Casanova", Force MD's who were also coming off a #1 record called "Love Is A House", and the third act was Glenn Jones who also had a #1 record. To be honest, all of the acts on the tour were a little hotter on the charts than we were, but that was all right because that was what we needed, a strong tour package.

I appreciated James putting The Bar-Kays together with these guys. I missed him on stage and I missed his friendship. He and I had a special relationship in the band. He was the bandleader when he was there but I was the lead singer, the focus of all the attention, the guy with the charming personality. I never had a real desire to kiss ass or do the kinds of things that were required of the leader, record label or radio personality. James loved it, and it was a plus for The Bar-Kays that he did. I was more about keeping the morale of the band up, keeping the show tight, keeping everybody looking like stars.

James hung out on the tour helping the promoter. It was awkward not having him on stage but we got through it and the tour did fairly well.

Later, I came up with the idea to have a Bar-Kays reunion jam session at one of the popular clubs in Memphis. We needed a boost in our morale and Memphis needed something to put The Bar-Kays back on her mind and on her lips.

The reunion was at the newly opened Memphis Nites Club. The club was packed with Bar-Kays fanatics and it was a magical night for Memphis. It was an extraordinary evening for me when about fifteen former members showed up, including James. Some of the guys I hadn't seen in years, much less played with them.

The magic happened again when James took to the stage. I don't remember being as happy as I was that night in a long time.

Some of the former members had not spoken to each other in years. After the show, we all talked, told war stories and reminisced about good times. It was an evening to be remembered.

We often carry stuff, grudges, malice, and other awful feelings around in our hearts and minds for absolutely no good reason at all. The boys in the band all needed this, and so did I.

21
Changes

In 1992, James came to the band and asked us to consider taking him back into the group. I had a big lump in my throat for a minute and then I told him I would think about it. At the time, the band was hot but it wasn't like we were mad at James, at least I wasn't. As the leader of the group, I agreed to let James come back. Harvey and Winston went along with it.

James came back as the bass player and to this day he has never left again. Shortly after James returned, Harvey left the group. I believe it was because he was just worn out with the lifestyle of the road and everything that went along with it. He married his longtime girlfriend and later entered the political field followed by a career in the justice and correction fields.

Winston soon left after getting a call to ministry. He became extremely active in the church and gospel realm. He also got married, returned to school and had kids. He recorded some incredible gospel jazz albums on his own label.

To this day, we all remain great friends but for some reason James, Harvey and Winston rarely talk. I can't quite figure that one out.

So there we were, James and Larry, back together again. Haunting me in the back of my mind was the fact that while James had been away from the band, he and Mark, the keyboard player, had gotten together and done a record called "Zero In July", which was not a bad record at all. James, of course, had the connection to get the deal done and Mark did the record. But there were horror stories floating around about how James had taken advantage of Mark.

Mark knew absolutely nothing about that part of the business and the two of them had stopped speaking, which was strange. I noticed that there were no concert dates or anything done while the record was out. I was hoping that James didn't have anything like that on his mind with me. First of all, it would never have worked because I was way too smart for something like that and the other thing was I was being unfair to James, assuming that he took advantage of Mark, not knowing the whole story. However, I knew James well enough to know that he took care of himself in whatever situation there was. He was just that kind of guy; he would say it was business.

Anyway, James and I took on the task of putting the band together, starting with replacing Winston. James and I knew that if we were going to continue with The Bar-Kays, we had to find guys who were considerably younger. It was a twofold situation. We would record new material and also keep a great funky band that sounded like The Bar-Kays. A younger group, we felt, would bring new ideas to combine with the experience the two of us had, and we also needed guys who respected the quote unquote "ole school." That was the criteria.

We hired Tim Horton on drums and Bryan Smith on keyboards to replace Winston. This was not the best choice but Bryan could do a lot of things that we needed done in the studio. We hired Michael Anderson on guitar, a really talented kid.

After getting all the slots filled with either permanent or temporary guys, we went to work on new music. Meanwhile, James was working his magic with the local label in Memphis connected with Select-O-Hits distributors, operated by Johnny and Sam Phillips, relatives of the famous Sam Phillips family who discovered Sun Records and a bunch of huge rock 'n roll and country artists. We signed a record deal with their label, Basix Records, in 1994 and released an album called "48 Hours." The first single and video was called "The Slide" which only went to #82 on the charts but was a big turntable hit and got us back working, something desperately needed because financially, things had gotten bad. I mean really bad.

Marie and I started arguing more about money. Holding up my end as head of the household was not happening so I had to take a regular job working at a community center for minimum wage. I totally hated the idea but I had to take care of my family, at all costs, meaning I had to swallow my pride and make the best of it.

One of my best friends had a sister who was the director at a Memphis community center for the Park

Commission. She pulled strings to get me hired immediately as a community center leader. Few people knew who I was because the centers were in the poor parts of town and only the directors of the centers were familiar and amazed to see me working there, and for such low pay. I guess they figured things must have really been rough.

As it turned out, once the word got around as to who I was other centers wanted me to be the director at their center. Pretty soon (against all city policy) I was working at about four or five centers at the same time, on all their payrolls, which made the money kinda all right.

More importantly, while working at the centers, I became close to a lot of the kids who were victims of single parent homes, verbal and physical abuse, and malicious staff. I became attached to many of them and got a lot of them to open up to me privately about their problems. I soon became known as "Uncle Larry" to many of the kids. I started a music class at some of the centers to help the kids who had talent and wanted to unleash. I received so many *Employee of the Month* awards that some of the staff members became a little upset with me. They couldn't understand why the kids enjoyed being around me and talking to me so freely.

I worked for the Park Commission for three years. Marie and I bought our second home while I was there.

Business started to pick back up for The Bar-Kays. My phone was constantly ringing. It became a big distraction and my superiors grew sick of it while hating on me at the same time, especially when I pulled up one morning in a new Mercedes. It made no sense at all to anybody, except me. A new home in a great neighborhood, a new Mercedes, and I continued to work with the kids at the Park Commission loving every minute of it.

I eventually had to leave the Park Commission, but I realized before I left what the Lord's intention was for me in all of this. He wanted to humble me, get me off of my high horse, and get me out of that which he despises, "pride" and allow me to understand that he would always take care of me if I would take care of my family. In the process, he wanted me to be a blessing to many kids who needed a father figure, someone to talk to, someone to look up to, and someone to trust.

Having a special needs child gave me the wisdom and understanding to help many of the mentally challenged kids that I had in my classes at the center. Kids who could not have made it in a regular school setting, mainly because the other children were far too cruel to kids like that.

The neighborhoods where I worked were some of the worst in the city with crime rates off the radar. Most of the time, there were no fathers in the households, and the mothers were on crack or were serious alcohol abusers. It was a horrible scene. I actually hated to leave, but I had to get back to being Larry Dodson, lead singer of the World Famous Bar-Kays.

22

Demons

I couldn't seem to drop the drug demons that persisted in my life. Even while I worked at the community center the dope men would bring me packages to keep me cool.

Back then we did a song with Evelyn "Champagne" King on the "48 Hours" album. It was a remake of "If Loving You Is Wrong." It was an idea of mine and it turned out well but it couldn't save the album. However, the "Slide" single caught the interest of Mike Curl who was over Curl Records.

Once again, James worked his magic, and he got us a deal that we all could live with. Mike didn't want an album with all new songs; he wanted a half and half album with half new songs and half old covers of some of our previous cuts. In essence, it was a "Best Of" album with some new cuts, meaning he wouldn't have to give us a lot of money for the project—and he didn't.

The album was called "The Best of The Bar-Kays" released in 1996 and our first single was a cool cut co-written by a local songwriter from Memphis. The song was called "Everybody Wants That Love". Personally, I liked it but it lacked that *it factor* as a song to put us back in the top 10 again.

By now, it's been a minute since The Bar-Kays had a legitimate top 10 hit. James and I are having a reality check that no label is going to pick us up with our track record getting worse. We had already had a label meeting with the record label that I absolutely hated with a passion, Malaco Records. They were a bunch of red neck, Ku Klux Klan type of white guys that had been taking advantage of black blues and soul acts and writers for years. I guess I should say it was not all of them but seventy-five percent of them fitted this description.

The one meeting we had with Malaco I walked out twenty minutes into the meeting because of the language and attitude of Tommy Couch, Jr. He was running the label then. He was a clown with absolutely no respect at all for black artists.

James was working for Select-O Hits as a promotion man, at that time. Malaco owned the majority stock in Select-O Hits so it was messy to deal with them. Johnny and Sam were extremely nice Christian fellows, and fair-minded. We ended up doing a lot of business collectively.

I ended up producing many projects for Johnny as the years went by, maybe fifteen or sixteen years. We continued to tour as much as we could, based on the fact that we were trying to get more money as a talent fee. Not being really hot, it was difficult.

In 1998 there were three different volumes of "The Best of The Bar-Kays" released, but we were not seeing or getting any royalties because we were not smart enough to booknote all of the stuff and peel the onion back as did the smarter artists. Meanwhile, my drug abuse and binging was getting out of hand.

While James was away, my drug binging would sometimes last two or three days. I would stay gone and not remember where I had been, or Marie would track me down at one of the drug clubs and come get me and take me home. I had plenty of money so I could get all I wanted. I would straighten up for a while and it would happen again. It was as if another person lived inside of me. That's what it's like when you're an addict.

After James came back, I slowed all the way down but the demons were still there. That was maybe the only time it came too close to Marie and our marriage, and rightfully so, she had taken all she could take. If she would have left me I don't know what I would have done because she meant the world to me. Finally, after being gone for a couple of nights straight on a crack cocaine binge I had come home and argued with Marie as usual. She left and went to work in the car. I was on the stairs crying and praying to God. I asked him first to forgive me for all the harm I had caused Marie and my family, and to take the taste and desire of any drug from my body. Then I asked him to make me so ill if I ever tried to use cocaine again that it would discourage me from even trying to get it again. After that prayer on the steps, my life changed.

Marie begged me to get back into the church. I can honestly say that I can't thank her enough for begging me to come back to church while I was in my addiction. It changed my life when I did. She told me to come and listen to Pastor Christopher Davis at St. Paul Church. She bet me that I would join after listening to him, and I did.

I knew that if I was going to give up cocaine I would have to give up drinking too because one made me want the other so I gave up drinking and I also quit smoking cigarettes.

I never went to rehab and honestly I backslid and tried to slip and take a toot at a party and just like I asked God to do, I got sick. I mean sick like I had never gotten sick before. It happened a couple of times but since then I've remained clean. I haven't even smoked a cigarette. I stopped drinking for about five years but now I drink champagne. Anybody who knows me knows that's all I ever drink.

God is good, but be careful of what you ask Him for; that's all I can say. I got back in church and God touched my heart like never before. We found a good church home in St. Paul Church, where we remain members today. I sing in the male chorus and ironically my youngest brother, Michael, is the Minister of Music there. Mike and I are the musical guys of the family out of four brothers.

After I got in church and swore off drugs and alcohol, Marie and I became closer than ever. It took some time for the trust to get back in place but we came to understand that drugs are a spirit and when you are under the influence of that spirit you are not the person you were, thus you can be forgiven for the horrible things you did when you were caught under that devil spirit. That's exactly what drugs are, the "devil's" spirit. I will never touch drugs again for any amount of money! Nor do I entertain people who indulge in that.

James and I started to realize we needed some help all the way around to get to the next level and energize the band to increase its value. We started to have conversations about looking for a manager. We quickly got hit with a reality check. Managers, especially good ones, were already with money making bands or artists who they felt would be the next big thing. We were neither. We had jacked off a year's contract with some big time guy in LA who did absolutely "jack shit" for us and we mutually parted ways with a letter.

There was one guy who caught our attention. He managed J. Blackfoot, an incredible soul singer who was once the lead singer of the "Soul Children", a vocal group that had a string of hits at Stax Records in the 60's and 70's. His name was Cato Walker. His mother, Mrs. Polly Walker, was B.B. King's travel manager, and her husband had been B.B. King's band leader, so Cato knew the ropes. Since B.B was with someone whose artist had worked 300 days a year, Cato knew what being busy was all about on a big scale.

After some thought, and a little reservation, Cato took the job of managing The Bar-Kays. James and I kind of knew what we were getting and mainly needed someone to help with the day-to-day stuff and to help out with sales on the books.

Cato didn't travel with the band unless it was absolutely necessary and we were cool with that. He had a day job working for a realtor on Beale Street who was a demanding guy. We knew him so we gave Cato a hall pass, so to speak.

Being the soft-hearted guys we were, especially me, I came up with the bright idea of a Bar-Kays' 30th Anniversary Reunion where we would invite as many of the pass players to come and perform in a big Bar-Kays band. We would donate a portion of the proceeds to our Bar-Kay's Scholarship Fund, which was supporting HBCU's only and in our city, Lemoyne Owen College.

Allen Jones' mother, Marjorie Barringer, was a career school teacher. After she retired, she was rather well off financially because she and her husband were quite smart and had invested well. They had land, pool halls, rental properties, you name it. She kept up with Allen's royalties from writers from many big records along the way for people like Isaac Hayes, Otis Redding, Johnnie Taylor, Rufus Thomas, The Dramatics, The Cop television series theme song, Bad Boys, just to name a few.

Marie and I took Mrs. Barringer for a Sunday drive. She wanted to see Lemoyne College and the projects across from the college, so we drove her to both. As she was in the back seat looking at the run down projects, she said, "Their kids will never have a chance to get into this college that's right across the street from them. They need help.'"

I asked her what she meant and what she wanted to do. She quickly said, "'Let's help them!'" We went home and started the dialogue about a scholarship fund of some sort. I remember her asking how much we (The Bar-Kays) were willing to put up. I told her that we would put up whatever she wanted us to and as often as we could we would match her donations.

She was half kidding. She knew she would be making huge donations and that we wouldn't be able to match hers, at least not as often, but she wanted to make sure we were serious. We decided to call it the "Marjorie Barringer Allen Jones Bar-Kays Scholarship Fund". We started it about 20 years ago with our first scholarship being given in 1996. Since then we have elevated to sending three to four kids each year to Lemoyne Owen College, and the list of graduates goes on and on.

Let me go back to the 30th Anniversary Concert. Cato helped us organize it. We decided on the famous Orpheum Theater for the venue. We would film and record the show and hire The Ohio Players and Brick as the main entertainment.

From the local side, we hired and invited a couple of local acts for political reasons, but they were good acts. We invited DJ Bobby O'Jay, the leading DJ in Memphis radio at the time, to be one of the hosts. He was an iconic figure in radio, period. We invited the Mayor of Memphis who was at that time the honorable Dr. Willie Herenton. He was an incredible mayor and a good friend of James and me. We would often seek his counsel on matters of importance to us and he would always give us solid advice, whether it was what we wanted to hear or not. He was a straight forward, no-nonsense kind of guy.

The white folks in Memphis feared Mayor Herenton because he was not afraid of them. He spoke his mind at all times on all matters, no matter who had to say ouch when he rendered his decision on an issue. We loved him and he loved The Bar-Kays. He was always front row at our concerts. His favorite Bar-Kays song was "Anticipation".

We also made a big deal about a super band performance by members of the original Bar-Kays and former members.

Turns out that Cato dropped the ball. He didn't have sponsors as promised and completely dropped the ball. To this day, we don't know what happened to Cato's envy concerning this reunion, but he sort of got lost toward the end as we got closer to the event. He stopped answering his phone about arrangements for the evening, and to know Cato was to know a guy who was thorough, an extremely sharp dresser, always had a good assistant, but on this event...crickets.

Luckily, James and I had just received a large royalty check and we ended up using all of it to pay for airline tickets, the souvenir booklet, and deposits and hotel rooms.

The concert was a huge success. The opportunity to see guys who had been in the band and had left for whatever reason was a real joy. We got a chance to hang out the night before the show. The City of Memphis awarded a few of us from the original Bar-Kays a famous "Note on Beale".

"Note on Beale" is an iconic award given only to special musicians from Memphis. We were all floating on air the entire weekend. We had a huge star-studded after party on Beale Street. It was one of my most memorable times in The Bar-Kays ever. Things were really looking up for me and the band!

23
Big Break

We got a huge break in 1997. Sinbad the comedian did a deal with HBO to do a series of live concert specials geared toward funk acts. There were three or four acts on each show but it was always the top acts. When we got a call to do a live concert on the show, we almost died. Our show would be filmed in Aruba and the money was very good. And guess what...we killed it. It was one of our best TV performances ever. In fact, HBO had a policy where they would send the video and audio files to the participants so they could fix whatever was broken, add the sound if they had a bad night, and do it all over again. We listened to our show a couple of times and sent the tapes back and told HBO to run it just like we played it that night. We didn't need to fix a thing. We were so proud of ourselves.

The band was made up of me, James, Michael Anderson, Tim Horton, Kurt Clayton, Ezra "EZ Roc"

Williams, and our background singers Robert Day, Cool Cal Taylor, and Karen Milam. As a vocal group they were known as 3-2-Da-Lef and they were da bomb.

Our performance on the show was only thirteen minutes after HBO edited it but it was a hot thirteen minutes of a musical intro, "Too Hot To Stop", "Holy Ghost", "The Slide", and "Freakshow". Besides the snake I was known for, I performed a fire trick which consisted first of me coming out on stage and saying 'too hot to stop.' I used hidden flash paper with a lighted cigarette between my fingers to ignite the flash paper whenever I wanted it to. It made it look like my hands were on fire. The crowd would go wild when I did it.

After the show-stopping performance on Sinbad's Summer Jam on HBO, The Bar-Kays were reinvented just like that. Our stock and booking price went up at the same time.

Keeping the same band combination, we continued to tour. We worked on new music at makeshift studios. We had sold all of the previous real studios to other clients. We sold Onyx Studio to the lady who we used to charter our buses from after we sold our personally owned buses. Later, we sold an incredible studio to Gary Belz of the rich Belz family which was later called The House of Blues Studio.

We released three more "Best of Bar-Kays" albums released in 1998. Around that same period, I started producing projects for various artists around Memphis. I produced projects for Johnnie Phillips at Select-O-Hits for Basix Records. Producing was a passion of mine. It felt comfortable being in the captain producer's seat or as we call it *behind the board.* I had the talent and patience to pull the best out of any singer or musician I was working with. That's the making of a good, solid producer.

In 1999, I was in the studio producing a project for Johnnie Phillips when I got a call from Bobby Harris of The Dazz Band asking for a meeting about joining in on an idea to do a project called "United We Funk All Stars". It would consist of a live album, a studio album, and a national tour performing as a super band with principal members of The Dazz Band, The SOS Band, Confunkshun, The Bar-Kays, and Charlie Wilson. It sounded like a great idea.

I didn't know Bobby Harris that well, but we talked and he explained to me that a rich guy by the name of Bo Bovard was interested in his business plan to start a record label and do a tour. Bovard had agreed to fund the entire operation, which was probably to the tune of well over a million dollars. The record label and tour would also involve Rick James and Roger Troutman. Unfortunately, and tragically, Roger was killed by his brother two weeks before signing the final contract for his deal.

James and I flew out to LA, as did the other principal members of the other groups, where we had a meeting and met Bovard. After we saw the label operation and plan for the tour, we signed on. We were the last group to sign an album deal with the label, which was called Major Label. To show our good faith and trust in them, we recorded the album and turned it in prior to getting our album budget. Of course it came through but we wanted to keep the album on schedule for them. They paid us well for the album budget and we got off to a great start.

Preparing for the tour was another deal. Everything was first class. Bovard brought in clothes designers and tailored three outfits for everyone. Mine were snake-skinned suits, of course. They brought in a shoe designer with hundreds of boxes of designer shoes to match each outfit.

The concept for the show was unique. There was no set change. We all played and sang with each other throughout the show and as one band finished a song, in a matter of seconds the principal members of the next group would be on stage backed by mostly The Bar-Kays throughout the night with a mixture of musicians from the other bands, so there was never a need for a set change.

There were three guitar players, seven horns, three background singers, two bass players, a percussionist, and electronic gear with sound effects. Ahhh, man! This was a band to die for. No one could touch us and no one wanted to once we started the tour.

Prior to going on the road, we wanted to go somewhere and rehearse and get it tight so that everyone would get use to the cues and learn how to move on and off the stage in a matter of seconds so the next act could be on before the audience noticed. We decided to return to Memphis where we rented a warehouse downtown. We brought everyone to Memphis for three weeks straight. We brought in a makeshift stage and a PA system, the closest thing to a night's performance. We put together one of the hottest shows on the road. Charlie Wilson helped a lot. I contributed a great deal because that's one of the things that I enjoyed. I have a talent for putting stage shows together. I always did it for The Bar-Kays.

For a period of three days I had not seen James at rehearsals. This was odd and he had been on my mind. I felt that he might be having problems at home but he and I always gave each other space and respect. We never ever interfered with each other's personal life. Of course, like all guys, we would vent at times but that's about as far as it went. Our personal lives were just that, our personal lives. Perhaps that may have been a curse for us because there were times for both of us when we should have talked about what was going on at home. Anyway, James shows up finally at rehearsal with his face all twisted and his skin dark. I almost fainted when I saw him. I asked him what was wrong and he told me it was Bell's palsy, a form of a stroke that happens to your face and leaves it in a twisted position. Sometimes people completely recover to different degrees. Immediately, I knew this was from nerves, tension, or something he was going through with his family. All I could do was pray for him. James was much stronger than I would have been because I could not have come around looking like he did but I guess he had no choice. Thank God, he eventually got better.

During this same year I decided to open my own booking agency. I did so with a little apprehension because I wondered if artists would trust me, being that I was an artist, too. As time went on I found it to be quite the opposite. I was trusted more because I *was* an artist and the fact that I was a band leader, and I had good relationships with most of the principal band leaders, I was trusted even more.

The agency was appropriately called La'Marie's Entertainment, the La from my name Larry and Marie from Marie's name. I made Marie president of the company because I was in a little tax trouble, a carryover from the early Bar-Kays and some from the new band. I thought to myself what better time to use my agency and help book the tour dates.

I found some promoters out of Charlotte, North Carolina. They would let us start negotiations at $35,000 to $40,000 per night there. Michael Parran and Charlie Wilson's camp, as well as Bobby Harris and his partner, Marlon McClain, all hated the idea of me being too smart to be an artist *and* an agent to book and contract tour dates. Now I see why. It was a glimpse of the shrewdness that Charlie's management would carry throughout his career to eventually not only put him back on top but to surpass all expectations anyone could ever have for any African American artist. At that time I couldn't see it. I thought they were hating on my company.

Charlie let his wife, Mahin, and his manager and son, Mike, kinda look after all of the business moves. The investors soon went away because Mike stalled the deal. Bo ended up sponsoring most of the tour dates. We opened in Atlanta with Kiss FM filming the first date. Actually, it was the second date because Bovard lived in Denver and wanted to get the show videotaped for him to look at it before going out. He asked me to do him a favor and find a good video shoot at a local club in Memphis, set up a performance, and let the admission be a can good for the needy so that it would be a packed house. It worked, and I paid for the shoot.

James and I helped set the show. We got great video footage for our press kit. Bovard got what he needed to look at and I got my $30,000 back that I put up to get it done. As it turned out, Bovard ended up paying for a lot of dates that lost money, including all our salaries. The deal was that all of the principal band leaders would get a $10,000 advance for signing on to the label and the tour. We were paid $1,000 a night salary. The band was paid around $400-$500 a night. For some reason the promoters didn't quite understand how the United We Funk All Stars Tour worked and the dates were slowly coming in so Bo sort of created dates for us to play with the help of Bobby and Marlon at the label.

Bobby, Marlon, and the rest of the guys running the label were spending hundreds of thousands of dollars keeping the label afloat, the offices open, and the tour on the road. They were steadily trying to sign new acts like Cameo who shifted them and never turned in their music after being paid, so the story goes. Then there was Rick James, which was a whole other story. We got as far as a promo-picture with Rick and that was like pulling teeth. The only way we got Rick to do that was to go up to his house where we found him sick with a very bad cold from jumping in the pool the night before. He had not been to bed. He was stoned to death but we finally got him propped up long enough to get a few shoots with the rest of the artists, and that was the end of the photo session.

Rick never turned in his music and he was never able to be a part of the tour because he fell ill and had a stroke. Charlie ended up getting a number one single on the label called "Without You", which was the beginning of his comeback to radio and immense popularity with the public. As for The Bar-Kays, we didn't get a record release while on Major Hits label but all in all it helped the popularity of the group for a while. We did record a live album in Detroit at Chene Park with Tom Joyner called "Tom Joyner Presents the United We Funk All Stars". It was a great live album. No one would ever believe that the night we recorded it, it stormed like a tornado was erupting. Today, I have no idea how we pulled it off with a sold out crowd that did not leave because of the rain. Luckily, it was a covered pavilion, but the rain could still get in through the sides because the wind was blowing so hard. Trust me, the Lord was truly on our side that night.

The album sold well and later we shot a video in Orlando with Tom at a live performance with United We Funk (UWF). Unfortunately, it was never released because of some contractual issues between Tom and the label. As time went on, Charlie was only able to do a few dates with us because his solo career had taken off so well with the success of his hit single. We understood but we missed not having him on the tours. He was a powerful part of the show when we did all of the Gap Band songs. The people went crazy, but because we all had so many hit records of our own we carried the tour well without Charlie.

Charlie was an absolute hoot to be around, and probably one of the most incredible voices I had ever heard. Mahin and Mike made sure no one got near him that might have any bad habits and entice him to backslide into some of his old ways.

We celebrated Charlie's fifth year of being drug-free at my home in Memphis. I had a huge six-bedroom and six-bath house. The entire tour came over and we had a big cake for Charlie. It was a nice celebration. Charlie had worked hard at staying clean and it paid off for him in a big way in the years to come. As I looked at Charlie blowing out the five candles on his cake, my eyes watered. Not for him, but at the thought of how God had truly looked over me, kept me throughout the years of my addiction, through all of the accidents I had from being out all night loaded trying to get home with drugs on me, and the police would find me in a ditch. I would have to call Marie and luckily for me they knew who I was and let me go.

My eyes watered because I recalled how God saved me from being killed when I totaled my car and I stepped out unharmed after trying to get home from clubbing all night. These are just a couple of the many times God kept me until he finally delivered me from evil drugs. I knew just how Charlie felt!

24

A Testimony

My booking agency, La Marie's, was really getting off the ground and becoming a good revenue stream for my bank account. I was gaining respect from old school acts as well as acts in other genres. I was picking up big accounts that really got me some recognition from other larger agencies. I always had the gift of gab and a good personality so that helped me with the haters who didn't like the fact that I was pulling this shit off as a booking agent while being the lead singer of one of the better and more respected bands on the road.

The Bar-Kays continued touring the U.S. and Asia, and in 2001 we released two more greatest hits albums, both of which did well and helped to keep the band's name on our fans' lips when they saw our album on the record shop shelves, whether it was a new piece or not.

We were working hard on new music, writing, and looking for new songs from any writer who had a good song. We were also looking equally as hard for investors to fund an entirely new project and a complete new overhaul of the group, including a brand new look, new stage show, new wardrobe, everything. As God would have it, we got extremely lucky again. James had a friend who lived in Houston, Texas. She was a young lady who had been married to a very successful football player for many years. She and James had been talking about investing a few dollars into the group for a return of course. James brought the idea back to me and I thought it was interesting. The family was well respected and not only was she a nice Christian lady but so were her brother and sister who all seemed to be in favor of making the investment. She and her husband were separated at the time so she was free to make the financial decision along with her siblings.

We found a young writer and producer in Houston to help co-produce the album. Archie Love, one of the singers in the band and one of my dear friends outside of James, went back and forth to Houston to record some cuts. We recorded some cuts in Memphis too with various students and soon we finished the album called "The Real Thing".

Prior to the album, I started my independent label, Right Now Records, but no success came to me with anyone on my label. On the other side, James had a label called JEA Records with a similar story— no success. We decided to combine our energies and join forces to form one label together called JEA/Rightnow Records. "The Real Thing" would be our first release funded by our Houston investors. We didn't have a distribution, and in my mind Select-O-Hits would be perfect, but James chose to do business with his longtime mentor, Al Bell. I believed this to be a bad idea. Al meant well but he was not properly staffed to keep up with accurate records, so our reports to our writers seemed weird, to put it miserably. It nearly broke up our company stemming from mistrust on royalty statements and accounting that we could never get on time from Al Bell's company.

Eventually, we parted ways with Al and tried to find a new distribution and some more music for a new Bar-Kays album. Meanwhile, our Houston investors were growing weary with us for not being able to get any return back on their investments. They really had nothing but good intentions with the loans so James and I made up in our minds to do all within our power to pay them back.

On JEA/Rightnow Records we had gotten up to five artists, which included the incredible voice of J. Blackfoot. I produced five albums on him, which included his last album before he died.

Of all of the artists on the label, J. Blackfoot was the breadwinner. His albums actually helped us pay the bills. We always managed somehow to keep a decent office and a studio operational at all times, allowing us to continually work on songs, whether we had funds to put them out or not. James and I always managed to come up with an investor to keep us in business.

James had a friend in Atlanta that invested into our company. This investment allowed us to finish recording and releasing one of our latter year's best albums, "House Party". It was the combined financial efforts of Donald Murphy, owner of I.M. Records and The Bellinger Family (our Houston, Texas investors) that helped to keep us in business through some lean years. For this, James and I, and the entire band, would be forever grateful.

The other artists were Archie Love and Lacee, and on our gospel label, Testimony Records, we had Perfection, an incredibly anointed young gospel group, and The Angelic Voices of Faith, one of the most popular choirs in Memphis and the Mid-South, which happened to be directed by my youngest brother, Michael Dodson, who was an amazing choir director with a pretty soulful voice.

Looking back, it's somewhat strange how James and I started Testimony Records. We had leased an office building in downtown Memphis on Second Street, mainly because James had purchased a home downtown and he thought it might be a good idea to stay close to the quote "money folks". We converted the space into a studio. I remember both of us being in the control room one day listening to some products we were planning to release when James told me that he had just returned from looking at a gospel act that was rather good. This was intriguing because I had just seen and heard an incredible gospel act, too. I realized that God was moving in both of our hearts to branch out to a gospel label.

I think both of us were hesitant about bringing the subject up for fear it sounded too farfetched. However, after a not so long conversation, we both sort of exhaled and openly talked about starting a gospel side of our company. When I tell you that the decision was not about money--it was not! It was a move that God inspired both of us to do because we both had a desire to help spread the good news of Jesus Christ and we both sincerely loved gospel music. That was seventy percent of what I listened to every day at the office and at home. Some of my all-time favorite singers were gospel artists.

We named the label Testimony Records. While dealing with this label and getting to know the gospel world better it brought James and I closer, and spiritually it was uplifting for both of us because all along the way this was a ministry for us and not so much about chasing a dollar.

Marie enjoyed the gospel label, the work we were doing, and the fellowship and ministry aspect of it all. She loves Gospel music as much as I do and she has always attended church on a regular basis.

25
Tour of a Lifetime

"The House Party" album was finished and released in February 2007. We worked long and hard on this project. James talked his son, record producer, rapper, and songwriter Jazze Pha, into writing and producing a cut called "Sho Nuff". I did several duets, one with the diva herself, Shirley Brown, on a strong cut called, "We Can't Stay Together". I did another song with a kid named Marcus Scott who is now lead singer for Tower Power. He's one of my favorite young singers. That song was called "Superstar". It was a challenge for me to not let him out sing me on my own song but it was a great expression for the both of us.

The young producer from Memphis who produced the record was J-Dav. James did an incredible job on the promotion side with a next to nothing budget. In my opinion, James is one of the top five promotion guys in the business today. He has always been underrated, kind of like The Bar-Kays. We were always swimming upstream to gain recognition from the industry where it really counted. We have yet to be called to perform or appear on the BET music slots, American Music Awards, or any of the tribute segments to old school or funk eras that these shows have frequently done. It is often disenchanting to see younger artists trying to pull off some of the old school segments on the award shows when they could have reached out to some of the real bands like The Bar-Kays, The Ohio Players, Confunkshun, or a host of other funk bands that are still performing at a high level.

I can pat myself on the back for taking over The Masters of Funk Tour, allowing some thirty Funk and R&B artists to perform twenty-five to thirty days a year through touring together. When I took ownership of the tour from what was originally called United We Funk All Stars, I went to work putting dates together through my booking agency and it began to work.

Some of the performers like Switch, Sugarfoot, Slave, Yarbrough and Peoples, Steve Arrington, One Way, Al Hudson, The Mary Jane Girls featuring Val Young, Brick, Confunkshun, and many others were not working on a regular basis for one reason or another. The fact remains that every act I just mentioned performed at a high level and have a great show even today. We have a great time together on tour every year.

In 2009, we landed a special series of concerts for the troops in Iraq and Kuwait. There was a lot of fighting going on at that time between the U.S. and Iraq and this was not a USO based tour. It was a special concert series of five concerts with The

Masters of Funk. The performing bands were The Bar-Kays, The Dazz Band, and Confunkshun. It was a life-changing experience for the group.

The Army would not reveal to us what city we were going to (for security purposes) until we were about to land and then a soldier would come on the plane and tell us where we were.

While there, I experienced days when the temperature got up to 125 to 130 degrees. I had never been in that kind of heat before, but the troops were used to it; they didn't break a sweat. We had to drink several liters of water a day and wash our hands constantly so we would not pick up any germs or diseases.

Archie Love and I documented everything. We hardly got any sleep for filming our own little documentary, which started from getting on the plane in Memphis to returning home from the trip. We visited hospitals and the wounded soldiers. We had closed meetings with combat generals who gave us the inside scoop of what was really going on with the war, not the CNN version but the truth. It was fascinating between what we heard from them and what was being shown and talked about on CNN and the news back in the U.S.

We visited command centers. To our surprise, we saw nothing but African Americans; yes young black men and women running the war.

We took several tours of the base where we were shown all of the wasted tax dollars spent on equipment that was never used because it was never needed. Probably the biggest lie we found out about was that there was far less fighting going on than what was portrayed on television. It was almost a joke. However, we did see, on a couple of occasions, helicopters bringing in wounded and sometimes dead soldiers from the occasional tough fighting that did go on.

As for the concerts, sometimes it was two hundred people, sometimes fifty, and then sometimes there would be seven to eight hundred troops depending on if the troops were on the base at the time of the concert. For security reasons, we were not allowed to leave the base. Personally, I never had the urge or desire to. We signed thousands of autographs while we were there.

While performing in Iraq, I watched some of the female troops crying during the performance because we were the first bands of this nature to come out in the field and perform exactly where they were. It was a rewarding feeling.

We would go back and perform for the troops two more times, once in 2011 and again in 2012. The last time we went, most of the troops were gone as the new president had promised he would bring them home. I am a witness that he did keep his word.

The last trip was very hard on me because of back problems that I had started to have. I learned I had sciatica and a bulging disc in my lower back, which made it difficult to wear the bulletproof body gear that was mandatory.

One memorable time for me was on our second trip. We had a chance to visit the Bin Laden palaces that had been taken over by U.S. troops and turned into bases and sleeping quarters for the U.S. Generals or guests from the United States. We took a tour through all of them. I saw the lake where he kept crossbred flesh eating fish. They used the lakes to toss and torture captured soldiers. They would throw them into the waters and let them be eaten alive.

Some of the palaces were still trimmed in pure gold. Others were replaced with a fake gold-like metal and the real gold had been removed at the request of Bin Laden. All in all, it remains one of the most memorable tours we played. We brought home 28 full video tapes of documentation of our three tours to Iraq. We plan to edit and release the documentaries in 2018 in different volumes.

Back in the states, our record label was growing in recognition as James and I struggled to help preserve what was left of the Memphis Soul and R&B legacy by providing a recording platform for some of the remaining artists and the new young up and coming artists like Archie Love.

Archie had a natural R&B, soulful voice and was a born entertainer. He had been a part of a group that had some record success on RCA. They were sort of understudies of The Bar-Kays at our production company. Little did I know, but Archie and his lovely wife, Lillie, would become two of my closest friends.

Archie was the one somebody in my life, other than James, that I could share anything with and could trust wholeheartedly. We became business partners in a couple of businesses that we still enjoy today and totally outside of The Bar-Kays. He was also as I often teased him, "Shop Foreman". Although he was never the band leader, he was always the elected guy to speak up on behalf of the band when there was an issue or when the band wanted to change a policy or wanted a raise. He helped the band grow up and start speaking for themselves individually when he stopped doing it for them, at least as much as he could.

Archie, and EZ Roc, the band's musical director and keyboard player, helped with all of the studio production and writing for the other artists as well as for The Bar-Kays. Although it got tough to get to James and to accept a song from the band, because the stakes were high and we felt more comfortable with a well-known producer, writer, or engineer calling the shots. Most of the time we never got a second chance to make a first impression at radio and in the industry. After four decades of music, we were still only as good as our last record, just like Michael Jackson and all of the others at this point in time in the music industry.

26

Parting is Such Sweet Sorrow

Growing up, I had incredible parents. Dad worked as a mechanic for a major truck line and for a few years my mom worked as an elevator attendant. They were honest, hardworking people and very much in love.

Dad was a polite and mannerable man who taught his sons to be respectful of everyone. We were taught and expected to say "yes, sir" and "no, ma'am" to adults, remove our hats when we entered the house or a building, open doors for women, be honest, and never lie about anything.

My dad prepared dinner for the family everyday that I can remember. Not because he had to, but because he enjoyed cooking. The only times I recall my mother cooking was during holidays, and even then she prepared only a dish or two along with a few desserts.

My parents loved to socialize and entertain. During the summer months they often hosted backyard parties. They would set up card tables, invite friends and neighbors over to the house, and my father would grill. Sometimes the parties would last all night long.

Of course my parents loved all of us, but I believe I received a little extra attention. When they entertained they would show me off by having me sing and dance. I realize now looking back on that time in my life that I was already a natural born entertainer. I was not shy; I loved to perform in front of people and the extra attention I received from it made me love it even more.

My mother was diagnosed with ovarian cancer in 1996 and she was a real trooper. She never complained. Not one day. She took chemotherapy and went into remission for 18 months but toward the end it was awful. She lost all of her weight down to about seventy pounds. There was a period just before she passed that she didn't eat anything for a month, and only took sips of water. She would wake up and I would be at her bedside, and she would ask why she was still here. I had no answer.

Mom was in hospice and the nurses were there daily so I asked them why she was still holding on. They told me that Mom was nervous about our father. You see, dad was suffering from Alzheimer's and it was so bad that he never knew Mom had cancer. He always told us that she was just pregnant. Bless his heart.

My other two brothers were going through serious drug problems so they were part of what the nurses felt Mom was holding on for. Worried about them, the hospice nurses finally advised me to gather all of my brothers and my dad and let each of them go in and talk to her, to kind of reassure her that everything would be okay and to let her know that we would take care of dad and each other. We all did that one day. Dad went in last, after all of us had our say. Mom had a glow on her face that day that I will never forget. It was a good day for her.

Mom didn't live but a few days after her talk with us. I was in the living room, on the couch, because at that point I had moved in to see after her. There was a friend of the family there who was experienced in matters like this. I had never seen anyone pass away. Mom was doing so badly that I prayed and asked God to take and release her from all of the pain and misery she was in. He did just that. Mom passed in 2000.

My brother, Mike, and I took care of dad for as long as we could until one day Dad didn't know who I was anymore. All I could do was look at him and cry. It was the strangest feeling I ever felt when my father didn't know me. I was just another strange face to him. Although I knew it wasn't his fault, it didn't help to ease my heartache.

I soon got over it and after a long search, Mike and I found a good home for dad. He grew progressively worse and became combative. I felt so sorry for him when I would see him crying because he couldn't make it to the bathroom in time and messed his pants. Dad was a proud man. He knew the nurses would have to change him, and his pride as a man was all over his face. Alzheimer's is a horrible disease. Dad passed in 2002.

Marie's father was next. He passed in late 2002. Her mother had already died of ovarian cancer in 1990. Meanwhile, my grandmother, Annie Mae Cole, whom I loved with all of my heart, was sick and getting worse. She had gotten to the point where she couldn't hold her urine or bowels anymore, and I was the only one taking care of her. I hired a nurse, then two nurses, then a live-in nurse. She, too, had Alzheimer's. She got so bad until even having the live-in nurse couldn't help to keep her from constant trips to the hospital for one thing or another.

Marie was so kind and understanding in this situation. She let me exhaust all of our savings, which was about $25,000 at the time, to take care of my grandmother. We finally had to put her in a home after she started seeing things in the house and seeing people who were dead. She passed in 2005. These were tough years for the Dodson family, yet....*the band plays on.*

27
Unsung

So one day I get a call from TV One TV Network expressing an interest in doing a segment of the TV series *Unsung* on The Bar-Kays. After weeks of going back and forth on scheduling, we agreed on times, dates, and interview locations which ended up being in Memphis for The Bar-Kays portion of the show. They shot over 48 hours of footage on us because the story was so intriguing and interesting and it covered much more history than they expected. As they began to interview us, after doing quite a bit of preliminary research on the band, they seemed to begin to understand just how unsung and underrated The Bar-Kays actually were and how big of a role the band had played in R&B, Soul, and Funk music, not only at Stax Records but in music period, having been around at that time for more than four decades.

It ended up being an amazing and revealing episode for TV One and their ratings went through the roof when our episode aired. After that, our business took a serious increase like the stock market when it goes up. People began to look at The Bar-Kays in a totally different light because they had learned things about the band they never knew. A whole new respect for The Bar-Kays emerged.

During filming, they were having difficulty understanding Ben Cauley, the surviving trumpet player, because he had recently had a stroke that left him with a speech impairment. James and I pleaded with them not to give up on getting the story Ben was trying to give them, and to be patient so that they wouldn't have to use closed caption while he talked and water the story down. They finally agreed and Ben got a chance to tell an amazing story—one that even I had never heard before. It was the story of how the plane that carried Otis Redding and the original Bar-Kays crashed, leaving all of them floating in the freezing lake. He could see and hear his fellow bandmates Ronnie the keyboardist, Carl the drummer, Jimmy King the guitarist, and others call out for help and their voices all slowly fading out and then he could no longer see or hear them. Ben cried all while he was being filmed. I cried when I saw and heard it for the first time, and every time thereafter, when I would watch that portion. Ben had never shared that story with us before. It was emotionally heartbreaking even after all of the years since the tragedy occurred. And then there was the sad scene they showed of Otis Redding's body being lifted up out of the water while strapped in the cockpit seat. Unbelievable!

Things started looking up again for the band. It seems there is just nothing like TV exposure, especially good TV exposure. We had been working on new material for a new album for more than three years on and off with guest artists like Doug E Fresh. He flew to Memphis after I called him to guest on the project, came to the studio, and blew me away with a one-take performance on a song he barely knew any of the lyrics to. He never wrote a word down. Not only did he not need paper to write or help him remember, but he double-tracked his voice on another track word for word without one mistake. My mouth dropped wide open. I had never seen anything like it in my life. On top of that, he refused to accept a fee for doing the feature. What an incredible friend. Not too many left like that.

George Clinton was another featured performer on the new product we were working on. It was a cut called, "What Goes in Da Club Stays in Da Club". We were playing in Mobile, Alabama at two different venues. Afterwards, I went over to sit in with George at the club where he was playing. After his concert, I asked him if he would do a guest on our album. Of course he said yes and asked me when.

The following weekend was Mother's Day. I said, "George I can't ask you to come next weekend because that's Mother's Day."

George said, "Let's do it now."

I said, "How are you going to get to Memphis?"

"How are YOU getting there?" he asked me.

I informed him my driver was taking me in a private car.

He replied, "I'll ride with you. Just pick me up in the morning when you get ready to leave."

I was floored. I didn't believe he was serious because at that time George was still getting pretty loaded.

The next morning, I go over to pick up George. Much to my surprise, he was up and ready to go. As we were leaving the room, he began throwing twenty-dollar bills all over the floor.

In amazement, I asked him, "Why?"

He said, "As I looked around at all of the homemade crack pipes and drug paraphernalia lying all over the place, when the maids come in if they pick up the money and keep it that would be stealing. That means they'll clean up the mess so I won't tell on them."

I was at a loss for words.

He got in the car and we drove to Memphis. It was me, the driver, George, and a lot of crack. We talked, George smoked, and I prayed we wouldn't get stopped, and we didn't. Long story short, we spent the weekend in the studio together, recorded the song, and George told me some amazing stories about his past, his adventures, his relationships with Bootsy and Prince. He shared with me the advice he had given to Prince when Prince would call him for answers about what to do regarding his music and contracts.

George was fascinating and very intelligent. There was not one subject that he could not hold an intellectual conversation about.

That weekend spent with George Clinton was priceless to me. To this day, George and Sly Stone are my most memorable sessions. They are both remarkably smart and talented men.

28
More In Store

At this point in time the band was well, but not performing as much as we would like. The main members now, besides James and I, were now EZ Roc Williams our MD and keyboard player, Mark Bynum on keyboards (back after being gone for more than 20 years), Archie Love on background vocal, and Angelo Earl (an amazing guitarist who played with us during the five years James was gone). As for the drummer's position and the other background position, we have moved guys in and out of these spots in hopes of finding the right guys.

We hadn't been to Europe or back to Asia in a while. We were so dependent on U.S. work and we didn't have a European based audience on the performance side. They loved our music, but the promoters were not sure if we could draw big live audiences because we had never performed there.

We were offered a two-week tour of Europe, starting with Paris a few years ago but we ultimately had to turn it down because we (being James and myself) were not going to make a dime after expenses. Looking back, and in retrospect, I should have taken it, gone over there, and knocked them out with the band and removed the doubt about the band's ability to still perform well and draw live audiences.

LaMarie's Entertainment was doing well and I started to get more dates on the "Masters of Funk" Tour, which I now legally own. I move twenty-five to thirty R&B and Funk bands around the country touring with this incredible show.

I later went on to create other tours like "The Lover's Delight", made up of single guy acts like Tony Terry, Glenn Jones, Michael Cooper, and myself as the "OG MC" but I also performed a couple of numbers. This tour was designed for ladies and lovers only. Then there was the Memphis Music Festival Tour, which I started. It consisted of William Bell, Eddie Floyd, Jean Knight, Booker T. Jones (leader of Booker T and the MG's), and The Bar-Kays. It was a total tribute to the wonderful iconic music of Stax Records. The audiences were 90% white but I knew it would be like that when I created the idea.

We also had a show that James and I particularly loved to do called, "The Bar-Kays Soul Revue" where we only played great music and songs from the Stax era. The people loved the show when we found the right audience. Younger age kids didn't get it or relate to it because it was music before their time. We played casinos, private events, white-based audience concerts and we killed them with this show.

I also created a tour called the Funky Divas and used all girls like The Mary Jane Girls featuring Val Young, CeCe Peniston, Shannon, Klymaxx featuring

Bernadette Cooper, Cherelle, Evelyn "Champagne" King, Anita Ward, Adina Howard, and others. I have a knack for coming up with hooks for tours. Getting them to sell is another thing, mind you.

My son, Larry Jr., has been my right hand man so to speak, and a voice of reason at times in helping to find ways to sell these packages and finding clients to sell them to. I got him interested in the bookings aspect of the business while he was in college by letting him intern in the office and learn how all of this works—contracts, agencies, dealing with the acts and different personalities. He still has some problems in some of these areas, simply because he is younger than seventy percent of the people he deals with and very head strong. But he's open to listening and that's the good thing about him.

Larry, Jr. became involved with helping kids further their education by running the day-to-day operation of the scholarship funds offered by The Bar-Kays Foundation. He now assists hundreds of kids with obtaining full scholarships to various colleges outside of the HBCU's that we support specifically. I'm extremely proud of him and so is his mom and his wife Syreeta, his daughter La'Rie (named after me and Marie). La'Rie is a straight "A" student and my plan is to help her get into acting. She's already filming her own kids TV show. She's truly an amazing young lady who I love dearly!

29

Once in a Lifetime

In 2013, we were able to get Jazze Pha to help us with a new record. It turned out to be a record that would turn our career around again. James and I, along with EZ Roc, went to Atlanta and got with Jazze and his team called the Unknowns. They came up with a cut called "Grown Folks". We all but did the entire record in one day, released the record on a deal we made with Bungalo Universal Records, and the record shot to #10 in the nation on the urban AC charts.

Behind "Grown Folks" we were now knocking down $25,000-$30,000 a night for our talent fee; the country loved the record. I did the storyline for the video and got some Memphis kids to shoot it and it served the purpose. It was a really good video which showed a much happier Bar-Kays. We were #1 in about twenty markets including Chicago. It was a Chicago PR Firm that got us in touch with our first African American president's people.

We beat out the Isley Brothers and O'Jays as choices for the entertainment at the Presidential Inaugural Ball for then President Barack Obama. It was a major performance for us. It was sold out and we were incredibly on point that night. Lucky for us, The Bar-Kays were invited back again to the White House for a special tribute to Stax Records with an all-star lineup. These are performances that artists would die for. I mean, you can't buy these kinds of priceless opportunities. We were blessed to get these performances.

I think it was finally starting to dawn on our peers that The Bar-Kays, unlike most of the Funk bands, were special and its history was different. The Bar-Kays were among an elite group of entertainers that helped to shape and mold music history.

We got another TV opportunity when we were invited to perform at the Trumpet Awards as part of a salute to the legends of Funk and R&B bands. Again, it was another chance to be saluted. This time with The Masters of Funk featuring Brick, Confunkshun, and The Dazz Band playing with an all-star band. It was a great performance and each band got a chance to play one of its biggest hits.

The Bar-Kays were again honored in 2015 when we were inducted into the R&B Hall of Fame along with Al Bell, Little Richard, Muddy Waters, Millie Jackson, Dorothy Moore, Sam Moore, Bobby Rush, Ike Turner, WDIA radio station, and a few more iconic artists.

Another huge surprise occurred in 2013. I got a call at the office from a filmmaker friend of my son's and a good friend of the actor, Louis Gossett, Jr. He wanted to know if we would be interested in filming

Lou's first show of a new internet series he was doing called "For What It's Worth" at his home in Malibu. Of course we said yes and arranged a time that worked for all of us. James and I went, along with my wife and son. I knew this was a once in a lifetime treat for all of us. We flew out to Lou's home. When we arrived, Lou's assistant answered the door.

The first thing I noticed when we entered into Lou's modest home was the hat that he wore in "Officer and a Gentleman". I got chills just looking at it and longed to put my hands on it. You see, I am a TV and movie fanatic. When I'm not working, all I do is watch TV and movies (plus CNN and the news).

Lou Gossett, Jr. and Cicely Tyson are among my all-time favorite actors. Lou was a warm and gracious host. We must have talked for hours before we started to film. It was as if he wanted us to know more about him before we shot anything. He was more open about his personal life than I expected. He talked about being banned from Hollywood because of his views on a lot of issues. This is what inspired him to start the internet series and give him a platform to talk about things he wanted to talk about uninterrupted and uncensored.

Lou also shared with us his bout with cancer and how the government tried to break him and take his property, which I did notice a "For Sale" sign in the yard when we arrived.

Lou was a Bar-Kays fan and that struck me as sort of odd. I guess I didn't expect such talented guys like Lou to have time for music, but it was quite different with him; he loved music.

When it was time to shoot the segment, everything went well. I noticed that Lou never had a script. Three fourths through the filming he said he was doing this all off the cuff. He wasn't used to using notes or pre thought-out scripts or questions. It was amazing at how professional it all felt and sounded. What an amazing talent.

We saw Lou again at the Trumpet Awards when he waved to me from the front row. He also came to the after party where we played. He did his best to be the host for our 50th Anniversary but he got called to a shoot with Halle Berry up in Canada at the last minute for a new TV series she had going on at the time, which I totally understood. What an amazing guy.

I have Keith O'Derek of Up Front Productions to thank for the introduction and setting up the film. In fact, Keith went on to become one of my favorite and most intelligent, resourceful, knowledgeable, and reliable film videographers that I have had the pleasure of working with. His company is a well-known film company in the industry.

Lou and I have remained friends from afar over the past few years, even though our work has kept both of us quite busy and perhaps from being even closer friends, I do believe. My son gets on me all the time because I am always so shy and humble when it comes to getting in touch with Lou. He would say, "Pops, please call Lou. He would love to hear from you. He loves the band and you especially and boom there Lou would be in the autograph line after a concert, trying to buy a CD or a T-shirt with that big wonderful smile on his face that would immediately get one back from me. What a guy!

30

And It Keeps Getting Better

James and I often talked about having a 50th anniversary. We knew it would take some planning and money to pull it off successfully, so we began to plan for our 50th anniversary concert.

Our publicist, Sheri Neely of the Neely Agency who has played a very important part in our career in the latter years, helped us put the 50th Anniversary concert together (and everything else in our career that followed as our publicist). Sheri is the only one we had in the last years before I announced my retirement. She was excellent.

While planning our 50th anniversary concert we were again honored by being inducted into the Memphis Music Hall of Fame. We were inducted with Carla Thomas and a few other iconic names in the music business. We were surprised that we were chosen when we were. We figured it would happen at some point, but not when it did. This was a prestigious honor for the band. Especially for James

140

and myself who actually were inducted along with Ben Cauley. I keep this award in the center of my mantle over the fireplace with maybe fifty other awards that either I have received with the band or I received apart from the band.

The Governor Lifetime Achievement Award is special and so is the NARAS Lifetime Achievement Award, given to greats like David Porter, Isaac Hayes, Steve Cropper, Booker T and the MG's, Al Green, and a host of other great performers and entertainers. I have a lot to be thankful for and a whole lot to be proud of.

Larry, Jr. always gets on me for being so humble and for seeming so unaware of who I am, as he says, or for not really seeming to comprehend or understand just how much The Bar-Kays mean to the music industry and especially to Memphis. I often reply to him and say, "I totally understand who and what I am but that's not what makes me tick." I make the joke to him sometimes that I have a home with six bathrooms and I have yet to find a way how to use more than one at a time. My point is that at one time it was a big deal for me to have an 18-room house like I have now with as many as six cars at one time, all paid for, a studio in my home to record as often as I please, but as time moves on my priorities have changed. I now try to concentrate on God more and try to listen to him so that it is He that orders my steps and not me walking or stumbling into every booby trap that the devil has set out there for me. My health, strength, peace, and the same for my family is what I now seek more than anything. The other stuff seems to fall into place when I seek God first. I know this to be true in my life without any doubt.

I wanted our 50th anniversary concert to have a purpose and so did James and Larry, Jr. who shares our passion for The Bar-Kays Foundation. In fact, it was through his efforts that we got our first $9,000 seed funding for The Bar-Kays foundation through a city grant awarded to us by the Shelby County Commissioner. The city began to take notice that once again The Bar-Kays was seeking another way to reach out through ministry to find a way to help those who simply could not help themselves, which was in fact, our mission statement for the foundation.

We decided to form a board to help raise funds through an ad souvenir booklet. It was comprised of a Who's Who list of CEO's, CFO's, and business owners from around the city. Larry, Jr. was elected as Chairman.

Larry, Jr., James, and I often didn't see eye to eye on matters, but at the end of the day we always managed to walk away from the table with a respectable agreement on issues.

We went back and forth on how much talent we wanted to have. Let me say, I guess I won that fight because we ended up with about fifteen guest artists, all of which donated their time and talent. The talent included great entertainers like George Clinton, Doug E Fresh, Confunkshun, Grammy award-winning The Dazz Band, The S.O.S. Band, Brick, Cherelle, past member of The Bar-Kays, just to name a few. There were other special guests like Al Bell, David Porter, and hosts were the actor Lawrence Hilton Jacobs and actress Elise Neal, who both did an excellent job.

We filmed it and before the end of 2017 we will have edited it down to present it to a major TV network in hopes that one of them will pick it up. We created what we call our Fab 5 Charities to donate part of the proceeds to. They were the Down

Syndrome Association of Memphis and the Mid-South, St. Jude Children's Research Hospital, Stax Academy School, United Way, and Lemoyne Owen College.

The expense to put on the event was staggering. Even though the talent was donated, the cost of flights, hotel accommodations, venue changes, sound, lights, backline, video filming, food, and other hard costs equaled to hundreds of thousands of dollars, which didn't leave much to be given to the various charities, but after all was said and done, we managed to present each of them a check. Praise God. They understood our dilemma and were not angry with us at all, knowing that we donated to all of them at some level on a yearly or bi-yearly level through one of our foundations or scholarship funds.

It was during the planning of the event that I personally started to reflect back on just how long I had actually been in the band as we were preparing the bio for the souvenir booklet. I also thought about how long 50 years of my life had been. I started to have small conversations with James, simply saying to him that I was a bit unsure as to how much longer I wanted to be on the road with the kind of schedule that I was keeping. With just me and him self-managing the band while I was running the booking agency full time, booking ninety percent of all of the dates we worked because we rarely got help from outside agencies, was rewarding but tough. I had started to go to New York periodically to sit down with various agency owners. James would go up sometimes and join me for lunch meetings and dinner meetings. Whatever we could arrange, it would help some.

I was really good friends with most of the agency owners but after we raised our booking price to

$20,000 as a starting fee and $25,000 to $30,000 in some instances, we stayed home more. The agency found that to be a hard sell for The Bar-Kays. That was only because they didn't want to roll their sleeves up, and it was easier to get $12,500. We finished with a deal.

I continued to contemplate more and more about the aspect of slowing down and just about working period. Perhaps, it was time for me to retire. I began to talk to Marie about it. We talked about perhaps both of us retiring and spending more quality time with our daughter, Precious.

I also talked to my second best friend, Archie, who I could be really honest with (about anything, more honest than with James even). I told Archie about the idea of getting someone to take my place, cutting a new record on the new kid, and doing a whole new number on the band. Of course, he didn't like the idea but he understood the *why* I was doing it part, when we were putting music out again on a somewhat regular and consistent level.

I removed all of the distractions from James so that he could fully concentrate on doing what he did best, promoting records. He didn't have to do anything pertaining to the band. I took all of that over purposely and delegated it to accountants and road managers for some things, and the rest I did. This was the formula that worked. It allowed James to help get "Grown Folks" to a top 10 record even though he had taken on a job at FedEx, mainly for the flying privileges which he needed, and the medical insurance which he and his family needed.

The last few Christmas holidays, for me and my family, have been spent in St. Petersburg, Florida in a particular area called Treasure Island, which we all fell in love with. For the past several years, we have rented homes in various parts of Florida, but St. Petersburg always wins out.

Marie and I have talked about it and have started planning on keeping our eighteen-room home in Memphis. We would spend seven months there while leasing a home in Treasure Island to spend the winter months, thus eliminating the winter forever in our lives.

As part of my retirement, I would buy a cabin cruiser boat, one that sleeps five to six people, and keep it in Florida along with one of the Mercedes cars.

The more I think about this, the more real it becomes. Each day I realize and understand just how important it is to spend precious time with my family at this period in my life.

31

The Best is Yet to Come

In 2017, I finally made my mind up to retire and slow down. I talked to James about it and it was a strange and uncomfortable meeting for the both of us. I wanted him to understand and believe that I wasn't walking out on the band nor was I trying to hurt or harm the band in anyway. I thought about it a lot and although it may have appeared to be an abrupt decision, it wasn't. I planned it where I would stay in the band for a nine-month period until we found a replacement, which was going to really be something.

James took it as well as could be expected, I guess, and he seemed to honor my decision to end my journey with the band. I found an incredible kid as an immediate choice to take my place and as time went on, so did James.

James and I had already talked about how much we wanted the band to see the two of us have it all together during the meeting. Never for one moment did we want to let them see us worried about the outcome of the band with Larry Dodson not there as the lead singer. Yet, I knew in my heart and within my spirit that it was time for me to move forward into the next phase of my life.

The meeting with the band went about as well as to be expected, too. There was a moment when we sat around the table in the conference room when I felt the band say without saying *what are we supposed to do without you.* It was hard to hold back the tears but I dare not let them see me 'not have it all together' at that point.

Next, I contacted the news media. I arranged a press release announcing my retirement at the end of 2017 to be put on the wire, along with the announcement that we were auditioning for a new lead singer for The Bar-Kays, starting immediately. The search was on, both in the U.S. and abroad.

After the press release was completed, The Bar-Kays left the country on a 10-day cruise with Tom Joyner, playing on two of those days. LaMarie's booked thirteen acts for that cruise. Marie and I stayed for the entire cruise, which we normally do if we have acts booked to perform.

While on the Tom Joyner cruise, I received one of the biggest surprises of my life in the middle of one of our performances. James stopped the band. I saw Tom Joyner and Frankie Beverly of Maze walk up on stage. Tom took the mic and started talking to the audience about a private conversation that he and I had the night before when I told him I was retiring. He said that his first response to me was "bullshit!" The audience laughed. Tom said that after I explained to him that Marie and I wanted to spend more time with Precious, our special needs daughter, that he understood and supported my decision.

The audience began to applaud and then my son and some of the other performers rolled a huge cake out from the wing. It was amazing! I was totally outdone. I'm hard to surprise. It took all I had to remain cool and collected, to say a few words, and get back to playing some music before the team started to roll. It was an amazing and thoughtful gesture.

When we returned home from the cruise it was crazy because we had a concert scheduled to play in Memphis on June 16, 2017. It would be my last performance in Memphis, and the last time for the fans in Memphis to see Larry Dodson perform with The Bar-Kays before my retirement in December 2017.

I did about fifteen radio and television shows, some with James but most of them alone talking about me leaving the group to retire and all that goes along with it such as finding who would take my place, what my plans were, and on and on. I had only seen Memphis this excited over a Bar-Kays concert once before and that was over the 50th anniversary concert, but Memphis was really on fire over this one.

Confunkshun was on the bill to open up so it was going to be a good show with a red carpet and everything. We changed the show around a bit and rehearsed so it was going to be on point. I even detected that the band and crew were excited. I guess because we don't play Memphis in big venues much and it's always a big deal when we do.

We got through the Memphis show with flying colors. It was a sell-out and a total success. I had never seen Memphis so ready to see The Bar-Kays and receive us like they did that night. It was a perfect, mistake free, one-hour set complete with some historic video footage that rolled with the show that went back as far as *Wattstax* and *Soul Train*. The audience had a ball looking and listening to The Bar-Kays of today while looking back on the nostalgic footage on the screen some of which was 35-45 years old (and we were 35-45 pounds thinner, too). It was good to see the look on their faces—priceless in fact.

The audience went absolutely wild over some of my performances that night. When I performed "Anticipation" I received a standing ovation. What a night! Confunkshun put on a great show and I was given some awards from the Senate and other organizations.

We did another couple of private concerts hired by some wealthy folks that ironically just wanted to catch the band before I left. They were some of the nicest people one could meet.

The Bar-Kays performed one of the concerts on the roof of a four-level mansion at a downtown Memphis home. I won't call the name but during this private performance, once again James stopped the performance and the owner had his server give everyone at the party a glass of champagne. I was presented with a solid gold bottle of champagne worth about $1,500. My mouth dropped open. Once again, I was reminded of just how much I meant to a lot of folks, especially James.

I have received numerous calls and emails from all over the world either congratulating me or begging me to stay with the band. Some of the ones where they were asking me to stay were very touching and heartwarming. I guess I never really thought much about ever seriously leaving the band before now. Knowing that this stage of my life is about to evolve into the next phase of my life and knowing the many lives I have touched along the way, makes me feel exceptionally grateful and pleased.

32

And the Band Plays On

Marie has also decided to enter the literary arena and we are writing a book called, "Keep Looking Up When It's Down". This book is geared toward parents of Down syndrome kids. When it's completed, we will both be busy on the book signing circuit. Our son has already started booking speaking engagements and book signing events.

I am working on a new show and a new stage production for The Bar-Kays while James is busy working on the possibility of a new record for them. James and I are determined to make this transition an exciting one for the fans, the promotion, and all of the booking agencies that will be looking through the cracks in the door, so to speak, to see if the new lead singer will be good enough to carry the legendary band through the rest of its career.

From a creative standpoint, I am actually getting excited and looking forward to working with the new kid in the lead singer spot, creating a new stage show, and designing a new wardrobe for the band for a fresh new look. I'm a showbiz guy, taught by the best, the idol maker Allen Jones. I live to do these things. It's my passion, only to be equaled by my passion for putting records together, which honestly over the last few years I had lost my passion for putting music together, mainly because we didn't have the proper funding to promote the records, and we didn't have the attention of the younger producers who could help us put the right kind of record together to compete on radio.

Lastly, with me making the decision to retire, a new record would only have prolonged me staying with the band, with my heart not really being there. That totally wouldn't be fair to any of us. A new kid can come in with a new voice and a new energy and reload the band's worth.

My journey with The Bar-Kays has been a great one. I've made a difference in the music business with our music spanning through 30 albums over 47 years, through thousands of live performances, through the sampling of our music, through our songs featured in TV and films, through our scholarship foundation that has assisted hundreds of kids to attend HBCU schools such as Lemoyne Owen College in Memphis, and through The Bar-Kays Foundation that simply helps those who cannot help themselves, and finally through our second label that has given artists a platform to get their music out to the public when no one else would give them a chance, to help receive Memphis music, and help to keep it alive in our hearts and souls.

I can say all of this with pride and toot my own horn, proudly, because I have helped to make a difference in the music business during my 47 years as the lead singer of The Bar-Kays. I have stood center stage in front of the funkiest bands in music.

This part of my journey may be coming to a close with The Bar-Kays, but I remain encouraged, optimistic, and eternally grateful knowing that God has kept me and The Bar-Kays throughout the years, through all of its peaks and valleys. I can now move forward to the next phase of my life knowing that *the band plays on.*

Words from Larry
Why I Decided to Retire from The Bar-Kays

About a year and a half ago, my wife Marie and I started to talk about getting a second home in Florida to spend the winter months of every year. I could live out my dream, which is to own a cabin cruiser luxury boat large enough to accommodate six to eight people. On and off we started to look for the home, the area in Florida, and of course the boat. This was going to be our retirement dream for later in life when we both decided to stop what we were doing. As time went pass, we started to talk more about our daughter, Precious who has Down's syndrome. We talked about her age and just how much we have been blessed that she has superseded all of our expectations since the doctors predicted she would not live pass her teens. All of a sudden it seemed that time started to mean so much more to me. I began to realize that my entire life had been spent inside The Bar-Kays with very little time for my family, even though they rarely complained and were very proud of me.

I'm now 65 years old, and when I look in Marie's

eyes now they seem to politely say to me, "*Will there ever be just you, me and Precious time?*" I came to the realization that she is absolutely right! Moreover, I also had been thinking and coming to the bittersweet realization that I have always found comfort in having people being able to depend on me, and in doing so I have now found myself overwhelmed with responsibilities. I'm a co-manager, the booking agent, the tour owner, the producer, the wardrobe designer, the show arranger. I'm Pops, Uncle Larry, the social worker, the best friend, and above all I'm Larry Dodson the lead singer of the mighty Bar-Kays. Notice, in all of the titles and responsibilities I listed is there any mention of my family or private life? *This is why I'm retiring.*

My band needs me, my fans need me, but my family needs me and will enjoy me more for whatever amount of time God allows us to be together. I must remain obedient to Him always. I thank my partner of 47 years, James Alexander, and the boys in the band for being as understanding as they could on this really tough decision. You guys rock.

The stage remains my paradise. The fans will always be team Bar-Kays, but I know that no one would have ever tapped me on the shoulder and said: *Larry, go spend the rest of your life with your family or you're doing too much slow down we got this.* It's just not like that. Everyone just wants more and I do understand that, but my journey is over and they must understand that...I believe they do.

Photographic Memories

(Sitting from left) Larry Dodson, Jr. w La'Rie Dodson, Syreeta Dodson
(Standing clockwise) Marie Dodson, Precious Dodson, Larry Dodson

Larry & Marie's Wedding Day August 21, 1970

Larry & Marie Renewal of Vows on 20th Anniversary

Lois Dodson and Otis Dodson (Parents) My grandmother, Annie, (L) and my father Otis Dodson

(L to R) Larry Dodson, with singer, Charlie Wilson, & James Alexander

(L to R) Jimmy Jam, Larry Dodson, David Porter, Kurt Clayton
Memphis Music Hall of Fame

The Bar-Kays 1971

James and Evelyn Alexander at Hard Rock Premiere

(Bottom left clockwise) La'Rie Dodson, Syreeta Dodson (Choreographer and Dancer for The Bar-Kays) Cierra Williams (Dancer for The Bar-Kays)
Red Carpet Interview

(L to R) Marie Dodson, Precious Dodson, Larry Dodson
Red Carpet/Memphis Concert

Larry and Marie Dodson at Hard Rock Cafe

(L to R) Larry Dodson and James Alexander Cannon Center Memphis

(L to R) Larry Dodson, James Alexander, Ben Cauley at Stax Museum

Larry Dodson, Jr.
Red Carpet

Larry Dodson mentors to Down syndrome kids

Larry Reading to kids at an elementary school

Larry Dodson talking to the youth at Carver High School

Larry Dodson with singer, Ginuwine

(Left to Right) Larry Dodson with rapper, Drake, & James Alexander

(L to R) Larry Dodson, Precious Dodson, Larry Dodson, Jr., Marie Dodson

(L to R) Precious Dodson, Larry Dodson, Marie Dodson

(Front L) Larry Dodson's first concert

Masters of Funk with Kathy Hughes on Tom Joyner Cruise

(L to R) James Alexander, Actor Louis Gossett, Jr.

Larry Dodson, James Alexander

Masters of Funk at Trumpet Awards
Karl Fuller from Confunkshun, Reginald Hargis & Jimmie Brown from Brick, Bobby Harris & Skip Martin from The Dazz Band, Archie Love from The Bar-Kays, Felton Pilate from Confunkshun, Larry Dodson from The Bar-Kays, Michael Cooper from Confunkshun, Robert Day, Angelo Earl & James Alexander of The Bar-Kays, Kurt Clayton from Confunkshun and Donnie Sykes from The Dazz Band

Larry Dodson and James Alexander "Suited Up"

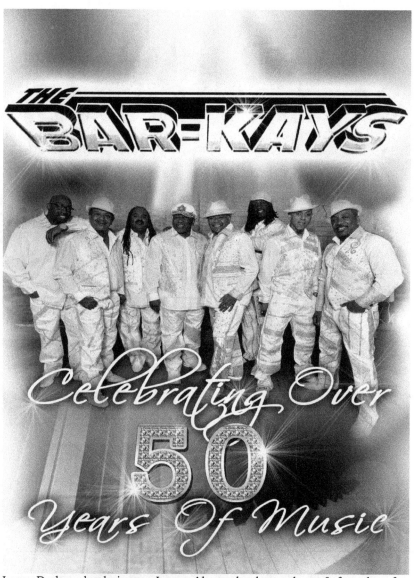

Larry Dodson-lead singer, James Alexander-bass player & founder of The Bar-Kays, Angelo Earl on guitar, Ezra Williams-music director (on keyboard), Danny Peterson on drums, Mark Bynum on keyboard, Robert Day-background vocals, Archie Love-background vocals

Drac From Slave in Rochester, New York

Sugarfoot performing with Masters of Funk before his untimely death

(L)

Bobby Rush and (R) Larry Dodson

Larry Dodson/Early Days

The Bar-Kays (L to R clockwise) Ben Cauley, Harvey Henderson, Michael Toles, Winston Stewart, Willie Hall, Larry Dodson & James Alexander

Larry Dodson performing with his snake

Rick James backstage with United We Funk All Stars in 2000

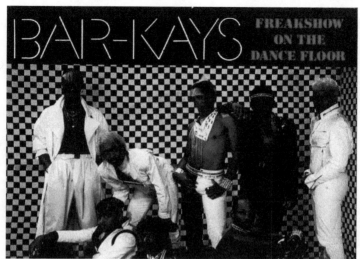

The Bar-Kays 12 Cover from Platinum Hit "Freakshow"

The Bar-Kays pose with a fan
Michael Beard, Marcus Price, Frank Thompson, Harvey Henderson
Mark Bynum, Reggie Pettes, James Alexander, Larry Dodson, special
fan from the show, Winston Stewart, Lloyd Smith

176

Bar-Kays in Iraq (2nd from left James Alexander, (R) end, Larry Dodson

Memorable Dates & Events

1972	The Wattstax Concert was the largest concert that we ever performed before in the history of the band
1973	The Bar-Kays Play the famous Whiskey A-Go-Go in Hollywood on Sunset Boulevard
1977	The Mothership Connection Tour with George Clinton headlining and Cameo with The Bar-Kays, co-starr was the biggest and most successful tours in the history of The Bar-Kays
1978	Awarded our first Gold Album by Mercury Records Alvin Hunter, the drummer on Wattstax, passes. Marcus Price, our guitarist, robbed, shot, and killed while preparing to leave for a tour with The Bar-Kays
1984	We were among the few groups on the last concert date before Marvin Gaye passed
1987	Allen Jones, our manager and producer died from massive heart attack
1986	James Alexander leaves the band for five years for personal reasons
1988	The Bar-Kays headline their first US Tour without James on bass
1991	James returns to The Bar-Kays Several of The Bar-Kays' long-time roadies, equipment, and production managers pass. Michael Young, Cazzell Bonds, Robert McKissick, Ray Love, Leroy Orange, Charles Stone and Cato Walker (Bar-Kays manager)
1996	The Bar-Kays 30th Anniversary Concert and Video Filming in Memphis, Tennessee
1980's	The Bar-Kays make the cover of Cash Box Magazine and Times.
1997	The Bar-Kays Film Sinbad Special for HBO
1996	The Bar-Kays get a Note on Beale Street
1999	The Bar-Kays begin tour with United We Funk All Stars
2000	We played the last concert with Johnny Taylor before he passed
2002	Touring with UWF and Charlie Wilson has a #1 Record while on tour
2003	Bar-Kays on tour Larry Dodson and James Alexander start their own record label JEA/Rightnow Records
2007	The Bar-Kays release "House Party" album and start the

	"House Party" tour
2009	The Bar-Kays Perform In Iraq and Kuwait for US Troops
2010	I take over "United We Funk All Stars Tour". I changed the name and trademarked it for ownership of the tour as "The Masters of Funk"
2011	Reggie Pettis dies – former background singer for The Bar-Kays
2011	The Bar-Kays Perform In Iraq and Kuwait for the US troops for the second time
2011	Drac, lead singer and lead guitarist of Slave, has heart attack and dies while on tour with the Masters of Funk
2012	The Bar-Kays Perform In Iraq and Kuwait for the US troops for the third time
2013	The Bar-Kays still touring but now with a top 10 single, "Grown Folks". The first top 10 single The Bar-Kays have had in over 10 years
2013	The Bar-Kays are invited to perform for President Obama's Inaugural Gala in Washington, D.C.
2013	Sugarfoot, the lead singer for The Ohio Players dies from a silent battle with cancer
2014	The Bar-Kays celebrate their 50th Anniversary in Memphis, Tennessee at the Cannon Center
2015	We played the last concert with Mel Waiters before he passed
2015	The Bar-Kays are inducted into the Memphis Rock N Roll Hall of Fame
2015	The Bar-Kays are inducted into the R&B Hall of Fame
2015	Ben Cauley, original trumpet player for The Bar-Kays dies from a heart attack in Memphis
2017	The Bar-Kays perform aboard the Tom Joyner Fantastic Voyage cruise and during the performance Tom Joyner and Frankie Beverly come on stage, and give me a farewell hug, speech, and cake along with the Masters of Funk, James Alexander, and my son, Larry Jr.
2017	My last performance in Memphis at the Cannon Center with The Bar-Kays before my official retirement in December 2017

And the Band Plays On

Photo Credits

Rodney Adams
Darren Catron
Mino Dillon
Jerome Ewing
Mike Kerr
Taylor Williams